The authors and publisher are not engaged in rendering legal, accounting, financial, or other professional services. If legal, accounting, financial advice, or other expert assistance is required; the services of a competent professional should be sought. This publication is intended to provide general, non-specific information. The advice and strategies contained herein may not be suitable for every individual. It does not cover all the issues related to the topic.

The accuracy and completeness of the information provided here and the opinions stated herein are not guaranteed or warranted to produce any particular results. The authors and publisher specifically disclaim any responsibility for any liability, loss or risk, personal or otherwise, which is incurred as a consequence, directly or indirectly, of the use and application of any of the contents of this book.

The authors and publisher have no personal connection or financial interest in any of the companies, services, or persons mentioned.

Although every effort has been made to ensure the accuracy of the contents of this book, errors and omissions can occur and websites and information can change or go out of date.

No part of this book may be reproduced, stored in a retrieval system, or transmitted in any form, or by any means, graphic, electronic, mechanical, photocopying, recording, taping, or otherwise, without prior written express consent from the publisher. The exception brief quotations embodied in critical articles or reviews, which give full credit and reference to this book.

Straightline Publishers, its logo (a light bulb in a black box), the Shortest Distance to Your Goal, TheSmartestWay, TheSmartestWay to Succeed, TheSmartestWay to Succeed Series, and Learn to Succeed TheSmartestWay are all trademarks of Straightline Publishers, LLC.

PRINTED IN THE UNITED STATES OF AMERICA

Copyright © 2008 Straightline Publishers, LLC
Library of Congress Control Number: 2008905574
ISBN: 1-4196-5683-X

The Smartest Way™
TO
SAVE

The Smartest Way™

TO

SAVE

Why You Can't Hang on to Money and What to Do About It

Samuel K. Freshman & Heidi E. Clingen

TheSmartestWay™ to Save
Why You Can't Hang on to Your Money —and What to Do About It!

By Samuel K. Freshman and Heidi E. Clingen

FIRST EDITION
Publisher: Straightline Publishers, LLC
"The Shortest Distance to Your Goal™ "
6151 W. Century Blvd., Suite 300
Los Angeles, California, USA
90045-5314
(888-524-8833)

Visit our website
www.TheSmartestWay.com

To receive your free email tips,
"TheSmartestWay to Succeed™ "
sign up at our website or email us at
Heidi@TheSmartestWay.com

What others are saying about "TheSmartestWay™ to Save"

"As a successful investment advisor over many years, I thought I knew all about making money, saving it, investing it, and spending it. But with just one reading of this book, Sam and Heidi have given me countless insights into improving upon the habits of a lifetime. If you take a few hours to read this book, you will enjoy the rewards over many years to come. It's like having your wise, rich uncle whisper in your ear all of the ways that he has succeeded in building and growing his nest egg."

–Alan Rudnick
Investment Advisor, Beverly Hills

"This book is an excellent tool for self and family intervention. It addresses how we tie money to emotions of all kinds and how that can lead to monetary self-medication and 'chasing' debt. It challenges the reader to identify rationalizations, minimizations, and intellectualizations that perpetuate the problem and in some cases, lead to devastating addiction. It not only addresses the problems, but offers outstanding solutions as well."

–Rick Zehr, Vice President
Addiction and Behavioral Services
Illinois Institute for Addiction Recovery at Proctor Hospital

"This book is filled with sage counsel and advice on common sense things that often go unmentioned."

—Gregory F. Sanford
Wealth management executive

"As someone who has listened to and learned from Sam, I can tell you this book should be required reading in Business School. Sam's straight talk on how we waste our hard-earned money hits the mark."

—David Bailey
President, Keller Williams Real Estate, Beverly Hills

"This is a must-read, especially in this economy. This book is the building block for acquiring true wealth."

—Grant Trauth
Authorized representative of Wealth Financial Group

"Sam and Heidi have done a remarkable job in bringing the topic of saving to a wide array of people. They have made the whole idea of saving both easy and fun through examples, tools and tips that help the reader achieve the goals set out in the book. I'm looking forward to the whole series of *TheSmartestWay*™*!*"

—Carol Allen
Family Endowment Partners, LP

"This book is concise, a pleasure to read and easy to understand, and very practical. Anyone who reads this book and follows the simple suggestions will be better off for the effort and on their way to financial independence."

–Kira S. Vincze
Attorney

"This is a no-nonsense, simple and straightforward manual on how to put your financial world in order. It offers great tips that are easy to implement on how to save money and take concrete steps toward financial security. Anyone who reads this book and follows the authors' advice will become financially healthy and a lot happier. Unlike other books of its ilk, 'TheSmartestWay™ to Save' has recommendations that are practical and doable."

–Andrew Bunnin
Vice President, Private Client Advisor,
major U.S. financial services company

"Some things never change. Will Rogers advised that if you find yourself in a hole, stop digging, and that the quickest way to double your money is to fold it and put it back in your pocket. 'TheSmartestWay™ to Save' incorporates and expands on this sage and timeless advice. It explains how and why to quit digging, how to start backfilling the hole, and how to smartly go forward and prosper. It contains good and timely advice for young adults starting out and for anyone who finds themselves in a financial hole, in addition to those who simply want to do better."

–Pat Bates
CPA

"This is a very useful book. It is jam-packed with good advice, some of which is surprising or shocking and the rest just makes plain good sense. There are so many ideas and techniques gathered here, the book will surely be valuable to people of various ages and economic situations."

—Gay Rubin
Author

"I have carefully copied your Principles of Financial Independence and sent them to my adult children. I just hope they take hold! My favorite is #9, 'The pleasure of luxury is short; anxiety lasts.' "

—Rick Reisman
Investor

"This is more than a book; it is a blueprint for financial independence! Sam and Heidi deliver down-to-earth money management strategies for life. From teens opening their first bank account to CEOs running their businesses, it contains pearls of wisdom for everyone."

—Melanie Pennell
CEO, Associated Ventures International

"Every individual is the architect of his own fortune."
–Appius Claudius

DEDICATION

We dedicate this book to our offspring,
Sam's four daughters and seven grandchildren and
Heidi's two sons.
May they all learn from this book
and lead a new generation of successful savers.

ACKNOWLEDGEMENTS

Book writing takes teamwork. We are grateful for the generous encouragement of our spouses, Sam's wife Ardyth and Heidi's husband Bill. We're glad for the friends and colleagues who reviewed drafts of the manuscript, including Lee Brown, Jan Brzeski, Heidi Neitert, Elena Schumann, Brenda Freshman, and our spouses. Sam's assistant Cindy Anderson and the staff at Book Surge have always given us prompt and professional attention.

Along the way, we have been inspired by "penny pinchers" and forewarned by "big spenders." We can never forget our parents and mentors who taught us to be thrifty and make the most of what we had, whether we had a lot or not.

We thank you all.

TABLE OF CONTENTS

PART III: YOUR MONEY AND THE WORLD

INTRODUCTION

"If you would be wealthy, think of saving as well as getting."
—Ben Franklin

We live in the richest country in the world, but many Americans are just living "month to month." They have trouble paying their rent or mortgage, their car lease payments and their credit card bills. Others may have a nagging feeling that they should be saving more money.

In our crazy, consumer-driven society, why are some people able to hang on to their money, and others aren't? This is a question that has perplexed both the authors for many years—even though we are as different from one another as any two people could be. We come from a different education level, social status, and religious background. We are different in our gender and our generation. But when we sat down to write this book, we found that we share the desire to help other people save and use their money wisely.

Two different perspectives

With this book, you get two different perspectives. Sam has had financial and business success as an attorney, banker, real estate investor, college professor, and author. Much of his success is due to guidance from his parents, mentors, and teachers. Sam's father, who was always there for his family and his community, taught him not to waste money and to search for value. Like his father, Sam has tried to help others help themselves and has mentored and advised others throughout his life.

Heidi also was raised by thrifty parents. She chose a less-lucrative profession as a writer. While it has not resulted in great wealth, it has been very satisfying. She loves to share her money-saving techniques on how to live well while being thrifty.

Who needs this book?

Everyone, no matter what their income is, wants to have more money. Therefore, this book has something for everyone.

In the last few years, Americans have collectively spent more than they earned after taxes. This means that their out-go is greater than their in-come. If they try to solve this problem only by focusing on earning more money—and don't control where they spend it—they will find themselves "running in circles."

Saving money is even better than making money— and a lot easier. That's because you don't have to go out and earn it—you just keep it!

Small savings over time result in big wealth

They say that the quickest way to double your money is to fold it in half and put it back in your pocket. But seriously, saving increases your money!

Slow and steady saving wins the race. The turtle will outrun the hare if the turtle perseveres. Small savings over time are more likely to create wealth than taking big risks. Use the magic of compounding interest to help you. If you keep time on your side, you can create substantial wealth.

Here's an example: If you start by saving just 1% of your income and you bring home (net) $2,000 per month, you would save $20 per month. Doesn't sound like a lot, right? Here's the good news: If you saved $20 per month for 20 years at an annual rate of 10%, you will have saved about $14,000. At the end of 40 years, you would have saved about $112,000!

Many people don't think about it when they buy something small but overpriced, like a $5 cappuccino. Take a close look at the small treats you buy for yourself. If you gave up just one $5 treat each week, you would have your $20 per month to invest and $14,000 more to invest probably well before you are ready to retire.

It's never too late to start

Small amounts grow to large ones over time if properly invested. Sam recently gave a donation of bank stock to Stanford University Law School. At the time of the donation it had a market valuation of $100,000. He had owned the stock for a number of years and originally bought it for only $100.

It's not too late to start saving. This book is as important for those who are starting out toward financial independence as those who are way down the path. Of course, the earlier you start the better, as it is much easier to save when you are young and don't have as many commitments and obligations.

No matter where you are in life you can start now to save and reach your savings goals.

Never stop learning

Heidi's grandmother once told her something that seemed puzzling at the time. She said, "The more I know, the more I know I don't know." When Heidi grew up, she realized that every day she can learn something new. Even the wisest person on the planet can always learn more.

Sam never quits learning. For example, he continues to add items to his list of Principles of Financial Independence, found at the end of this book. He likes to share what he has learned. He has shared this list with hundreds of people, and it has helped many achieve financial security. You can cut out the list and put it in your wallet or tape onto your mirror. It is kind of a "cheat sheet" map for your path toward financial independence.

Practice makes perfect

Now that you have purchased this book, you are entitled to a free subscription to our email tips, "*TheSmartestWay* to Succeed™." These are quotes and comments that will encourage you to reach your goals. There are three ways you can get your free subscription: Fax us the form at the back of this book, email us at **Tips@TheSmartestWay.com**, or subscribe online at our website **www.TheSmartestWay.com**.

Our goal for you

If you are reading this book, that means you are determined to change the course of your future. We wrote this book so you can learn to enjoy saving money. Instead of gaining pleasure from spending money, you can learn to get pleasure from saving it. By being thrifty, you can save enough money to invest wisely and become financially independent.

Our upcoming book, "*TheSmartestWay*™ to Invest" will help you earn money by teaching you how to invest the savings you will make by following the suggestions in this book.

More inflow than outflow equals happiness

We also want you to be happier. If your income is $1,000 a month and you need only $900 per month, you will be happy that you have $100 left over to invest or spend as you wish. You have avoided debt and managed your income responsibly. On the other hand, if your income is $1,000 and you need $1,100 per month, you will be unhappy because you don't have anything left over. You will continue to fall more and more behind.

As Charles Dickens wrote in *David Copperfield* more than one hundred fifty years ago, "Annual income twenty pounds, annual expenditure nineteen six, result happiness. Annual income twenty pounds, annual expenditure twenty pounds ought and six, result misery."

In other words, if you spend less than you receive, you are more likely to be happy. But if you spend more than you have, you will be unhappy, because overspending puts you into debt.

As someone once said, "If your outgo exceeds your income, then your upkeep will be your downfall." Instead, you need to learn to be thrifty.

What it means to be "thrifty"

Perhaps your parents or teachers told you to "save for a rainy day" and "pinch your pennies." That's being thrifty! To be thrifty is to be economical, spend wisely and save your money.

Thriftiness isn't just for average people. Some billionaires are thrifty. For example, Jim Walton, of

Wal-Mart, worth $18 billion, drives a 1999 Chevy pickup. Warren Buffett, worth $57 billion, lives in the same house he bought for $31,500 almost fifty years ago.

You can enjoy life and save at the same time

We all know how to shop and be consumers. Unfortunately, many people don't know how to save, invest, and build financial security.

This book will show you techniques to live life fully and also cut back on spending at the same time. Also, if you have money left over for long-term use, you will have a better life.

Some people spend much of their free time thinking about shopping and how to spend money. Sometimes they think they are "saving" when they shop. Unfortunately, most of the time they are just spending.

Other people devote their spare time improving lives, instead of spending money. They visualize how good their life will be when they are finally financially independent. They have learned the game of *not* spending their money—and enjoy it. They have learned to be the winner of the game, and you can, too!

It's not how much you make;
it's how much you keep.

PART I

YOUR MONEY AND YOU

Chapter 1

SOME QUESTIONS TO ASK YOURSELF

"Any fool can waste, any fool can muddle,
but it takes something of a man to save,
and the more he saves, the more of a man does it make of him."
—Rudyard Kipling

You become a better man or woman when you handle your money well. To help you do that, throughout this book we will show you how to use *TheSmartestWay*™ questions to help you make the best decisions.

Why are some people rich, but still broke?

You may know someone who makes you wonder, "He makes so much money! Why does he always seem broke?" Believe it or not, it's not difficult to spend beyond your income, even if it's a large income. Why? It's just a matter of more zeros at the end of the balance sheet.

On the other hand, some people with modest incomes have built great wealth. How did they do it? They knew the secret: It's not your salary that makes you rich—it's your saving habits.

It doesn't matter how much you make—or don't make. As Sam and accountants like to say, "It's not how much you make—IT'S HOW MUCH YOU KEEP."

How do you manage your money?

Saving money is a day-to-day process. Small, daily decisions add up to huge, long-term results. What is your savings goal? Do you have a savings account that would provide for your needs for three to six months? Do you have enough for a down payment on a house?

Can you manage your money better? Here's a little quiz to find out. Take a moment to answer the twenty questions below.

1. Do you take advantage of tax benefits, such as 401(k) s, IRAs, etc.?
2. Do you avoid using check cashing machines or ATM machines?
3. Do you usually pay off your credit cards each month?
4. Do you save at least 10% of your gross income in an emergency fund?
5. Do you avoid late fees and overdraft charges?
6. Do you usually pay with cash instead of credit cards?
7. Do you feel secure about your finances?
8. Are you a comparison shopper who shops with a list?
9. Are other things in life more important to you than shopping?
10. Do you balance your checkbook?
11. Do you buy gifts in an appropriate and cost-effective way?
12. Do you have a plan for supporting yourself with your investments?

13. Do you have control over your budget?
14. Do you make more than you spend?
15. Do you know your total debt? Is it a small amount?
16. Do you resist the temptation to use a debit card?
17. Do you handle your own finances?
18. Do you agree with your children and spouse/significant other on how to handle money?
19. Do you know how you are going to afford retirement?
20. Do you have enough insurance to protect your health, your possessions and your loved ones?

What do your answers mean?

If you answered "no" to two or more of these questions, you need this book!

You need this book to help you think about how you spend money and to give you techniques to help you make your money work for you. You are reading this book to learn to save and accumulate the money you need to invest. You believe that there is a way to achieve the financial independence that you have always wanted and that you deserve.

What is financial independence?

You are financially independent when you have enough income from your investments to live the lifestyle you want without working another day in your life. This amount depends on your location and your lifestyle. For example, if you live in Manhattan, you'll spend more than you would if you live in a rural area of Montana. If your lifestyle requires a penthouse, you'll spend more than you would if you live in a more modest home. Other factors to consider are your age, your health and how long you expect to live. Calculate your location, lifestyle and lifespan and add in variable factors, such as inflation.

Fortunately, financial independence can happen on a relatively small income. You simply need your monthly income to exceed your monthly outgo—for the rest of your life. Financial independence isn't just a matter of saving and being disciplined. It's also a matter of investing well, a topic that we explore briefly later in this book. Financial independence is the scenario in which your income from investments supports your lifestyle.

Before you learn to invest, you have to learn to save. Some people get confused about this. You can't invest unless you get out of debt, stay out of debt and save enough extra funds to invest. This is the path to financial independence.

Who is the servant and who is the master?

As Francis Bacon said, "If money be not thy servant, it will be thy master." P.T. Barnum added many years later, "Money is a terrible master, but an excellent servant." Which do you want to be, the master of your money or its slave?

You may have "toxic debt." Toxic debt is debt that is used to pay for something that produces no income and meets no real need. It also can be debt that produces income, but the income is less than is required to pay off the debt. Toxic debt will mortgage your future and prevent you from reaching your lifelong dreams, such as home ownership or a secure retirement. Toxic debt creates anxiety and stress and conflict in your relationships.

When you save enough and get out of debt, you will eliminate the need to rotate credit cards, post-date checks, or write uncovered checks. You won't be asking others to help "bail you out." You'll be more honest and gain more respect from others. Your broken relationships will start to heal. Instead of worrying about money, you'll give your job and your loved ones the attention they need.

When you rid yourself of toxic debt, your mind and body will improve. You may have fewer stress-related illnesses and deeper sleep. The discipline you exercise in controlling your money will create new "mental muscles" that will help you discipline yourself to establish a healthier lifestyle, both financially and physically.

To eliminate toxic debt may sound difficult. But it can be done if you use self-control. This little phrase can encourage you: "If you save your money, it will save you."

What are your priorities?

People can be strongly influenced by what they read in magazines and what they see on television. This can turn their priorities upside down.

Do you own your possessions? Or do your possessions own you? Do you fill your life with things that have real value for you and truly enrich your life? Or are your possessions stealing the time and affection that you should give your loved ones?

Your relationships with your friends and loved ones should be your top priorities. They enrich your life more than all the money in the world ever could. Nevertheless, your money situation affects your relationships. When you create enough funds to provide for yourself and your loved ones—for a home, college, retirement—you are keeping your relationships your top priority.

To be truly successful, get your priorities *and* your money in alignment.

What is the meaning of success?

It's unavoidable. You need to learn to save and spend wisely to be successful in life. Success is a matter of choices. We live in a great country. Here, we all can decide what we want to achieve and then make it happen. If you have money, you'll get where you want to go, faster. Small sums, saved and invested, become large funds through the miracle of compound interest.

Even if you pledge to give everything you have to others, as Mother Theresa did, money still helps. Freedom is a wonderful thing to have, and it's a wonderful thing to give. The more financial resources you have, the more you will be able to help others and share your freedom with them.

The most popular question

For over thirty years, Sam has been lecturing at various universities and colleges on Principles of Financial Independence and participating in mentoring programs for young businesspeople and professionals. The question people ask Sam most often is, "What is the most important thing you learned to become financially successful?" The answer always is, "It's not how much you make—IT'S HOW MUCH YOU KEEP.

It's not your income that makes you rich;
it's your savings habits.

Chapter 2

WHY ARE YOU IN DEBT?

"Money talks
–but all mine ever says is 'good-bye.'"
—Anonymous

Are you in debt? Does the amount of your debt make you uncomfortable? Have you ever thought about why you are in debt?

We live in a consumption-drunk society that operates on the belief, "I want what I want—so I should have it now!" For years, credit and debt have been relatively easy to acquire. As a nation, we have become accustomed to being deeply in debt. We are bombarded by consumer advertising that urges us to buy things we don't need and, sometimes if we think about it, we don't even want. These things keep our real goals in life out of reach.

Know how you got into this situation

You have to examine your thinking to find out how you developed your bad spending habits. Look at the roots of your feelings of blame and resentment, guilt and low self-esteem. Here are some of the reasons you may be in debt.

- You may be overspending to impress others. You may lack the confidence to say to your family and friends, "I want a new [car, house, widget], but I need to wait until I can afford it."
- You may be purchasing gifts you can't afford, in order to buy your significant other's love or your children's gratitude and forgiveness. You may be substituting gifts for love. Perhaps your parents tried to buy your love when you were young.
- You may feel that you work hard all day and you deserve to reward yourself. The media is full of messages encouraging these indulgences.
- You may be feeling lonely or unfulfilled. Face it, it's easier to go out and buy something new rather than to build relationships or accomplish your goals.
- You may be addicted to shopping. Perhaps your constant desire to go shopping is a way to distract yourself from doing what you should be doing to improve your life and genuinely increase your self-esteem.
- You may be worried about the world's problems and determined to just "live for today," no matter what the cost.
- Your family may have taught you to overspend. Childhood programming is difficult to change unless you acknowledge it.
- You may be convinced that debt is inevitable, that you are never going to get ahead anyway, so why try?
- You may still be rebelling against parents who "pinched their pennies." To compensate for a

deprived childhood, you may drive yourself to acquire things that you feel you deserve.

Look at this list and think about why you are in debt. If you don't understand it, you can't control it. If you don't heal these inner feelings, it won't matter how much money you have. You need to get your thinking right before you can get your finances right.

Understand the mechanics of money

To be truly successful financially, you need to save and spend wisely and understand the mechanics of money. You need to know where it all goes, whether it's disappearing through inflation, taxes, or your weakness for the influence of corporate advertising.

If you can anticipate the factors that take away your money, you can outsmart these situations by planning ahead. Then you can save enough to invest successfully and reach financial independence.

Plan for the speed bumps on the road of life

The best policy is to expect the best, but plan for the worst.

Life can come at you fast sometimes. Murphy's Law says, "Anything that can possibly go wrong—will!" Sam adds, "Murphy was an optimist!"

Job loss, divorce, illness, disability and accidents can create financial distress when you don't have enough funds set aside. What you need is a funding buffer, a savings account that protects you like the bumper on your car.

Don't make assumptions

Some of you have wealthy parents or family members. You may believe that you will receive an inheritance eventually.

Unfortunately, "your" money may not reach you if it runs into a roadblock. For example, your inheritance may be only hinted, implied, or assumed. You could have a "falling out" with a family member. Your parents could remarry and/or live much longer than expected. The money that you were expecting for an inheritance maybe used to pay for your parents' long-term medical care needs, to pay for estate taxes, or to recover from financial downturns.

Do you know specifically when the inheritance will arrive? Do you know how much might be? In any case, prepare for possible disappointment. Never count on an inheritance. Above all, don't spend it before you get it. (This is a good motto for all expectations.)

Later we will show you that windfalls such as inheritances are not for spending. They are a boost on your quest for financial independence and for creative capital to invest.

"Put your own oxygen mask on first"

We all want our lives to be meaningful. We want to help those who are near and dear to us. Nevertheless, you must take care of yourself first, before you can help others. Think about it. You can't help others if you are in trouble yourself. On airplane flights, the attendants remind us, "Put your own oxygen mask on first." This well-known phrase is a good way to remember this principle.

Keep your money safe. You can help protect others with it later, after you have reached your financial goals.

Reduce money stress

Here are some things you may do that can get you stressed about money:

- Listening to media hype and deceptive advertising

- Signing up for too many credit cards, debit cards and lines of credit
- Running up the balances on your credit
- Consolidating your debt with a disreputable credit counselor
- Buying a more expensive car, stereo system, wardrobe, etc., than you need
- Buying a larger home than you can afford

Money stress can force you to make quick choices that you regret later. Usually, decisions made under stress are not good decisions.

Be happy with fewer things

When you see something you like, ask yourself, "Just because I like it, does that mean that I need to own it?"

If you don't need it, don't buy it. A life of simplicity and freedom from endless material wants can be liberating. An added bonus is that you have simplified your finances and freed up more of your money to invest in things of lasting value.

Develop the habit of saving

Your savings can start small, but the rewards of saving are infinite. Find the inner motivation, the genuine desire to change your life for the better. Your commitment will be energized by visualization of the improved life that you'll have.

Einstein defined insanity as "doing the same thing over and over again and expecting different results." So start doing something different—and learn to hang onto your money!

It's not what your money makes of you;
it's what you make of your money.

Chapter 3

GET FREE FROM DEBT

"If we command our wealth, we shall be rich and free.
If our wealth commands us, we are poor indeed."
—Edmund Burke

I f you command your wealth, you command your life. Here are some ideas to help you become debt free so you can get your life back.

Cleanse yourself of toxic debt

Toxic debt is poison. It constricts your financial wellbeing by burdening you with interest payments, fees, and dependence on further debt. Toxic debt also prevents you from investing and achieving financial independence.

For many of you, your debt is working against you. You many feel like you are swimming against a rip tide of toxic that is pulling you down. Even if you understand this, it still may be hard to stop incurring more debt. When you want something you cannot afford, it's easy to think, "I'll just put it on the credit card."

You may be "living large" now, while you are racking up debt. You may be keeping up with your friends, family and neighbors. But they may be spending beyond their means too, and you could all be quietly sliding down the road to ruin together.

In any case, if you keep up your current level of debt, you will not have enough money left over to invest in your future and create financial independence for yourself. That's why we will show you how to control your debt in Chapter 9.

Protect your credit rating

You may be handling those "easy, low, minimum payments" every month. But what if something happened in your life that made it difficult to make those payments? What if you lost your job, got injured, sick, or divorced? What if the interest rate on the credit card was increased?

If you are late on your payment, the credit card company has the right to "dial down" your credit rating. This is very serious. A low credit rating, also known as your credit score, could prevent you from getting a loan or buying a home.

Find a role model

Is there someone you know who handles their money well, who has money left over at the end of the month? Maybe it's a friend, relative, co-worker, church member, or club member. Tell them that they have been an inspiration to you. Find out if they will give you some advice or mentor you and support your efforts to do better.

Ask someone to hold you accountable

There is nothing like accountability to help you eliminate bad habits. Choose someone you trust to hold you accountable. Tell that person your savings goal.

It could be, "I'm going to buy only one latte per week this month," or "I'm going to put $100 in my savings account at the end of each month," or "I'm going to pay off all my credit cards by the end of the year."

Give that person permission to ask you periodically if you achieved your goal. Write the goal down on a piece of paper, tape it to your bathroom mirror and look at it when you brush your teeth twice a day. This helps you set the goal in your mind as a top priority.

The Game of Not Spending Money

Make not spending money into a game. You need to win the game of "Not Spending Money" and outsmart your compulsion to spend.

Like any game, when you earn points, you feel a thrill of satisfaction. This game should be no different. Therefore, we suggest that when you reach each goal, give yourself an appropriate reward, based on how hard the goal was to achieve. To get motivated, make a list of rewards that would be fun or feel good—but don't cost money. Some examples of no-cost rewards are taking the time for a hike in the woods, relaxation in the bathtub, or a picnic under the stars.

Reveal your goals and your planned rewards to your loved ones and your mentor. They will encourage you and celebrate with you. Whatever you do, don't spend yourself back into debt when you celebrate!

Dream of the day when you will be able to pass on the favor and mentor someone who, like you, became snared in debt, but with your help broke free.

Become more introspective

Don't go crazy with anxiety about your financial situation. Instead, sit down in a quiet place and fearlessly and honestly confront yourself about how you handle your money. Admit your weaknesses, bad habits, and temptations. Realize that you are not able to outspend your friends and neighbors. Face your fears of being rejected if others found out about your true financial situation. Ask yourself *TheSmartestWay*™ question: "Why do I care so much about what other people think of me?" (Newsflash: you are thinking about them more than they are thinking about you!)

Now, ask yourself, "How can I use my money to help myself and my loved ones in a way in which I can be proud?" By doing things the right way, you can set a positive example of financial responsibility that others can benefit from and for which they can respect you.

Make your financial life more manageable

Money has become so very complicated. Make it simple again. Here are some suggestions: decide who— you or your spouse/significant other—should handle the household finances. Consider hiring a bookkeeper for a modest fee if neither of you is good at it nor has time. These changes will simplify your finances and help prevent paying overdraft fees and late charges.

Understand the Money Machine

The Money Machine is Heidi's name for "big money." Massive financial institutions and banking conglomerates control how most of the world's money operates. The Money Machine is the mover and shaker of global finance. It has functioned rather freely because, until recently, the public has been generally unaware how money works.

The Money Machine knows how to manipulate consumers to spend—and overspend—for the sake of convenience. Here's an example. Banks design their savings and investment products to offer convenience, such as ATMs and debit cards. But there is a cost for that convenience. One of those costs is overdraft fees that are automatically deducted from your account if you spend more than the amount in your account.

The fees are small, but mighty. In 2007 alone banks raked in a whopping estimated $17.5 billion from overdraft fees. The Money Machine knows that a little bit from a lot of people can add up fast!

The average consumer is the "little guy" compared to the Goliath of the Money Machine. It's understandable to feel out-maneuvered and manipulated. But with education, everyone can regain control of their finances.

Resolve to "beat the system" by its own rules. Tell yourself that when the Money Machine designed the system, they didn't plan on consumers as smart as you!

Watch over your money. Don't give it away freely. Otherwise, if you're not careful, your money will sprout wings and fly away, only to be sucked back into the vast void of the Money Machine.

Avoid debit cards

Debit cards make you lose control over your bank account. If you and your spouse/significant other withdraw from the same bank account throughout the day, you easily could become overdrawn and bounce checks all over town. It may be better to have separate accounts or mutually decide before each purchase.

Learn about "positive debt"

Debt can either work for you or against you. Some kinds of debt can work for you. If a debt is increasing your cash flow, it is called "positive" debt.

One suggestion is to use a low-interest rate loan to pay off high-interest debt. Here's one example: Say you have a large debt on a credit card that charges you 18% interest. If you could get a loan from the bank at, say, 8% interest and pay the credit card off, you would have automatically saved yourself 10% in interest payments. This could be a significant savings.

Here's another example: Say you have $10,000 in the bank earning 3% interest. You also have a loan for a car, on which you are paying 6% interest. It makes sense to take money that is giving you 3% and use it to pay off a loan that is costing you 6%.

In other words, if you have debt or a loan at a higher interest rate and you can get another loan at a lower interest rate, you can pay off the higher rate loan with the lower rate loan. Or you can use a loan at a lower interest rate to buy something that earns you a higher interest rate. Either way, you can save large amounts of money in interest payments that you didn't have to pay.

Control your money consumption

Some people go over their budgets very carefully each month—others just go over them! It's easy to spend more than you have. The question is how do you get your budget under control?

One trick is to think of spending money like eating food. Steal a tip from people who lose weight. Dieters are advised to keep a "daily food diary" to monitor what they eat. Do the same thing with your money consumption. Keep a "daily money diary." This will show you how much money you are spending each day, when and where.

Put a small piece of paper in your wallet or carry a notepad in your purse. Every time you buy something, jot down the details of the purchase. You could also enter it in your PDA. Yes, it is inconvenient to make a note of every purchase. But that's partly why this trick is helpful: it makes you stop and think each time you buy something. You may even be less eager to spend money because you know that you will have to log the purchase into your "daily money diary."

To break a habit, you have to first notice when you are doing it. If you spend money unconsciously, without thinking about it, it has become a habit. A "daily money diary" helps you notice when you are spending so you can learn to control your behavior.

The "daily money diary" also helps you see exactly how much you spend on those little "budget-busters" every week. Do this for a month. Then use the list to help you establish a monthly budget that realistically meets your needs.

Keep a small wallet

Here's another trick related to dieting. You may have noticed that if you have a larger plate, you tend to take more food. And if you put a large portion on your plate, you tend to eat it all!

The same concept of the size of your dinner plate applies to the size of your wallet. Keep a small wallet. Don't carry more cash with you than you are going to need.

As an experiment for one week, reduce by 20% the amount of cash you usually keep in your wallet for weekly spending money. At the end of the week, you will probably have managed just fine. Now you can save that money every week. It will start to add up!

Get on a cash-and-carry basis

Here's how to do it: First, list all the things you can use cash to purchase, such as groceries, haircuts, lunches, gas for your car, clothes, entertainment, etc.

Second, put the amount of cash you have allocated for each month in each category in its own separate envelope. Be sure to include a small weekly allowance for "walking-around" fun money or spending money. You need some spare money for the occasional treats such as beverages and grooming items. But once that weekly allowance is spent, you must wait until next week to treat yourself again.

Third, resolve to quit using debit cards, checks, and credit cards. You and your spouse or significant other must promise each other that you will not use your credit card anymore. The only conditions in which you would use the credit card are (1) if it is a planned purchase that you both agree on together, or (2) if you were 100% committed to paying off the entire balance that month.

Extra plastic on hand can make you feel like you have extra money on hand. This is not true. Credit is very, very expensive money. Use it only in an emergency. If you can't pay the card off at the end of the month, you can't afford the purchase. Try to remind yourself, "It's not money; it's plastic—and it's toxic debt!"

It's easy to get "hooked" on credit cards. Credit card addiction can sneak up on you. Before you know it, you may start "tossing down your plastic" several times a day. It's not until you get your monthly credit card statement that you finally realize what you are doing to yourself.

When you get "unhooked" from credit card addiction and use cash to pay for things, your friends will be curious. They will wonder how can you be so prepared and disciplined to be on a cash-and-carry basis. Simply explain to them that you are living within your budget and they can do it, too.

Control your thinking

Debt is a state of financial insecurity that can make you anxious. Freedom from debt is a state of financial security that makes you feel great!

Your goal of financial freedom will seem impossible until you learn to control your thinking and start believing in yourself and your ability to overcome your circumstances. To survive in today's tumultuous financial environment, you must resolve to be a "thrivor," not just a "survivor."

Affirm that you can "beat the system" that has tried to beat you. Systematically pay down your debts, save for investments and start enjoying more peace of mind and confidence. Adopt the attitude that you can get yourself back on track and win the lifetime money game.

Control your saving

Formulate a realistic plan to save, even if it's just a few dollars a month. Starting out small is okay. The goal is to develop the habit of saving. Gradually increase the amount you save. Most people should be saving at least 10% of each paycheck for an "emergency" fund.

The larger the savings, the larger the results. Strategic, disciplined savings can have enormous, long-term benefits.

Visualize your future

It's liberating to save enough money to be debt free and to invest. It's such a relief to be free from the anxiety and guilt of being in debt. Here's how to visualize yourself taking back control of your life. When you have a few quiet moments, close your eyes and imagine yourself accomplishing the first small, easy steps. What will it feel like to look at your bank account balance and see a large amount? What will it feel like to see your billing statement with zero due? What will it feel like to cut that credit card in half? Let yourself feel the pride and relief. Remind yourself often what that feels like.

It's not how much you own;
it's how little you owe.

Chapter 4

"HAVE-TO," "WANT-TO," AND "NEED-TO" MONEY MANAGEMENT DECISIONS

*"If your desires be endless,
your cares and fears will be so too."*
—Thomas Fuller

Learn to want only the things you truly need. Here's how. Every decision can be placed in one of three categories: "have-to" decisions, "want-to" decisions, or "need-to" decisions. First you need to be able to separate a want from a need. Learn to distinguish the difference between something that you need to survive from something that you simply desire.

Understand "have-to" decisions

"Have-to" decisions are decisions about what someone else wants us to do, or which you think you need to do because someone else expects you to do it. Do you worry too much about what other people think about you? For example, would you say to yourself, "I 'have to' buy that new car or house—or I will feel embarrassed around my friends." Sadly, it's human nature to judge others by their possessions, rather than by their character.

Whenever you hear yourself think, "But I *have to!*" stop and ask yourself, "Do I *really* have to?"

News flash: other people are not thinking about you as much as you think they are. They are too busy thinking about their own problems and themselves.

You may have heard the phrase, "He who dies with the most toys wins." Unfortunately, there is no way to win that game. Why? There will always be someone who has more toys than you. The game that you can win is this one: save, invest, and get rich. Here is the irony: If you're so busy competing and trying to appear wealthy, you're actually ruining your chance to become truly wealthy.

Understand "want-to" decisions

The next level of money motivations is "want-to" decisions. These are decisions about things that we want, often for personal pleasure or comfort, temporary satisfaction or to relieve some stress or disappointment. Have you ever said to yourself, "I bought it because I wanted to. I know I couldn't afford it, but I wanted it anyway." Look at "want-to" decisions carefully. They are seldom rational.

To spend needlessly on "wants" puts you behind on your investment program and derails your track to wealth.

Understand "need-to" decisions

The last and most important level of motivation is "need-to" decisions. What is necessary to meet your life goals and care for your loved ones? You need to pay for your basic need of food and shelter (appropriate in relation to your income) and to save for investment, retirement, your children's education, and unexpected emergencies. You probably have life goals that require investment in yourself for future reward.

Everyone has had the unpleasant surprise of broken major appliances, unplanned car repairs, costly dental work, or medical tests. Someone close to you may need long-term medical care someday. Medical expenses can crack your retirement nest egg, if your health deteriorates. Health care costs are rising all the time and people are living longer than ever. Put all these possibilities together, and you can see that saving your money wisely is a "need to" decision.

To categorize a purchase as a real "need," you must have a clear understanding of your own definition of "have-to"s, "want-to"s and "need-to"s. A good test is to ask yourself *TheSmartestWay*™ questions: "Is this the best use of my money? Can I live without this? Do I really need it to improve my life?" Keep your real needs uppermost in your mind. This will help you resist the "have-to"s and "want-to"s, and help you focus on the "need-to"s.

Don't catch "the wants" virus

Don't have endless wants. Learn to want only those things that you truly need. Constant longing for something you can't have or shouldn't have can make you miserable. Heidi calls this misery "the wants" virus. You have "the wants" virus when you say frequently, "If only I had [fill in the blank]."

Even if you finally get what you think you want, you may be surprised that it isn't what you really wanted after all. You may have heard the warning, "Be careful what you wish for—you might get it."

Develop "savings muscles"

Everything we do in throughout our day is based on inner decisions. To make the best decisions, ask yourself *TheSmartestWay*™ questions: "What are my real needs? How should I be meeting them?" Dedicate your energy into reaching your savings goals and taking action that will help you achieve it.

Exercise your "savings muscles." Like exercise, the more often and continuously you do something, the easier it becomes and the stronger you become.

Analyze your "money messages"

Most of us have unconsciously adopted "money messages." The sayings we keep telling ourselves without noticing. Here are some examples of money messages: "I don't know how to save because my family never did, or never could." Or, "I'm going to just spend all my money while I can and after I'm gone, everyone else can sort it all out." Or, "I avoid managing my money because it's: too boring, too hard, too overwhelming or too confusing." Or, "I would rather read the back of a cereal box than my bank statement."

You have to change the messages you tell yourself about money. This will help you take responsibility for your financial life and control your destiny.

You may have subconscious prejudices against people who have more money than you have. You may believe deep down that you don't want to be like "them." You may have opinions about other people and their money, such as, "Rich people think that they are better than everyone else." Or, "Rich people are not to be trusted." Or, "Rich people are unhappy because money can't buy happiness." Rich people are no different than anyone else in these areas. They are no better, no worse.

Face the fact that you need to be financially secure to achieve your goals in life. If you take a more mature approach, you'll get ahead faster.

Understand your money motivations

How you think about money may depend partly on when you were born. People raised during the Great Depression of the 1930s think differently about money than those raised during the Baby Boomer Generation. The Generation Xers and the Millennial Generation also have their own approach to money.

Regardless of your age or how you were raised, you are influenced by the same emotional factors about money. It's natural to want to buy things to gain acceptance, if you're insecure. You may hope that if you could just look and act rich, you'll feel rich. You may be tempted to try to "buy" love. You may dream that a "perfect" gift would heal a cherished relationship.

Pride and revenge are ageless motivators. You may secretly vow, "Someday, I'll show them!" You may want to hurt others or shame them with your money. But stop and think about it. If you waste your money, you're only hurting yourself, not them.

Be reasonable about your money decisions

Let's face it. Some money decisions aren't reasonable. For example, a recent study found that many people aren't interested in learning how to save and invest. This just doesn't make sense: Why wouldn't people want to have more money?

One reason we are confused is that our consumer-driven culture is so seductive. Manufacturers of consumer products conduct massive research to find out what products we think we want or we believe we need. Then they lure us into buying what they want to sell us. As consumers, we all are exposed to hundreds of marketing messages every day in magazines and movies, on billboards, television and the Internet. Advertisements are everywhere, from park benches and shopping carts to the sides of buildings.

Too many people are obsessed with the "art of the sale," the all-consuming hobby of shopping—what they bought, where they bought it, how much they paid for it.

Unfortunately, your money will eventually disappear—and you won't know where it went—if you're always thinking about spending your money instead of saving it.

Remember Sam says, "It's not how much you make—IT'S HOW MUCH YOU KEEP." Resolve to be an independent thinker, who buys only those "need-to" things that are best for you.

It's not the "have-to"s or "want-to"s;
it's the "need-to"s.

Chapter 5

BE CREATIVE AND SAVE MONEY

"The habit of saving is itself an education;
it fosters every virtue, teaches self-denial,
cultivates the sense of order, trains to forethought,
and so broadens the mind."
—T.T. Munger

If you want something badly enough, you often can find a way to compromise and get it inexpensively and yet effectively. You can learn it helps to be creative about getting what you want. Here are some examples from Sam and Heidi's lives.

You can have a room with a view

When Sam first started practicing law, his goal was to have an office in Beverly Hills. But he couldn't find "a space for services" arrangement, exchanging his time working for a lawyer for office space. (This was how most young lawyers started back then when they did not have enough money to rent an office.)

He did, however, find a firm that had a large, windowless storeroom. It rented for only $25 a month, compared to $100 for offices with windows. When he bought his office furniture, he asked the store decorator for advice. The decorator suggested installing drapes across one of the walls to give the impression that a window was behind the drapes. This worked fine, and Sam created a presentable office that was within his budget.

From this experience, Sam demonstrated that sometimes you can have what you want (at least almost!) if you are willing to be creative.

You can have a dream

While studying at Stanford University, Sam and his roommate dreamed about a tour of a major motion picture studio. In those days, the only way you could get onto a movie studio lot was if you knew someone who would give you a private tour. Sam's roommate's mother worked for a studio and she tried to get them a tour, but she couldn't.

Still, Sam was determined to figure out how to get a tour. He wrote a letter to the top executives of each of the three major studios in Hollywood. The letter explained that he was writing an article for the Stanford University newspaper about the influence of motion pictures on college students. He asked for an interview with each studio head and a tour of their studio. All three studios sent him back a pair of private studio tour passes. The heads of two of the studios each granted him a personal interview. He sent them copies of the article after it was published and received access to the studios again the next year.

From this experience Sam learned, "If you can dream it, you can do it."

You can strategize and negotiate

Here's something most people don't realize: you can negotiate with your home insurance company. For example, you can often negotiate with the insurer to settle the amount of the claim and not actually use all the money they give you in reimbursement for living expenses.

Many home owners' insurance policies have a "living expense" coverage feature. Your home could require repairs that may be paid by your insurance policy. In that event, you may need to move out of your home while the problem is repaired. If that happens, your insurance may pay for your living expenses during that time up to a certain amount.

A friend of Sam's had an 8,000 square foot home in Malibu that was destroyed in a wildfire a few years ago. He wisely had purchased sufficient coverage on the home. The owner was able to show that the rental fee for a similar home would be $10,000 a month. It was estimated that it would take eighteen months to replace the destroyed home and therefore, the insurance company would have had to pay $180,000 in reimbursements for living expenses ($10,000 per month for eighteen months).

Many of his neighbors had similar losses from the fire. They chose to use their relocation reimbursements to live in expensive hotels while their homes were being rebuilt. They spent months living luxuriously, but in the end had nothing to show for it. Sam's friend had a better idea. He met with the insurance company and negotiated a settlement of $150,000 in cash for his living expenses. He then bought a trailer for $20,000 and placed it on his lot while the house was being rebuilt.

He put the remaining $130,000 into investments. These investments would produce for him an income of $10,000 a year for the rest of his life. As part of his estate, he will pass on the $130,000—which at the time of his death will have grown into about $1,000,000—to his grandchildren.

The friend and his wife had worried that it might be difficult to live in the 800-square-foot trailer while they waited for their house to be rebuilt. To their surprise, they found the smaller quarters to be very convenient.

You can have elegance on a budget

We believe the special events in your life—whether they are anniversaries, bar mitzvahs, first communions, baptisms, quinceaneras, even weddings—can be fabulous, without depleting your savings account.

For example, about twenty-five years ago, while Heidi was studying journalism in San Francisco, she and her first husband decided to get married. They were determined to prove that with some planning, a small but elegant wedding could be created with a limited budget.

First, Heidi spent $100 on ivory satin and georgette fabric, lace, and ribbon so her mother-in-law-to-be could sew her long wedding gown. The invitations and stamps for their small wedding cost $100. They had found the perfect wedding/reception site, a rose garden arbor amphitheater overlooking the San Francisco Bay, at a cost of $50 to rent for the day. The trellises and roses were in bloom, so no more flowers were needed to decorate the site. The minister's fee was $50. (Today the fee is usually $150 to $300.) The groom's tux was $50. The best man and the maid of honor each wore their own best clothes.

The day before the wedding, Heidi bought $50 of fresh roses at the discount flower market to form her bouquet, the boutonnieres, the floral headpiece for her veil and to decorate the cake, which cost $50. The simple cake and champagne reception served a case of champagne that cost $50. The grand total for their entire wedding was only $500, but they received many compliments.

While prices are higher now than they were twenty-five years ago, the total cost for a small but elegant wedding could be less than $2,000. For example, the gown can easily be purchased for less than $500. You could budget another $500 on the bride's accessories or a bridesmaid's dress. With the remaining $1,000, you could spend an average of $100 for the invitations and stamps (print them yourself), $100 for the groom's tuxedo, $100 for the wedding/reception site, $100 for champagne, $100 for the cake, $200 for flowers and bouquets, $300 for the minister's fee. Remember, your wedding doesn't have to cost a down payment on a home. With planning and creativity, you can have a simple but lovely wedding and reception that everyone can remember with pride and pleasure.

It's not what you do;
it's how you do it.

Chapter 6

DEVELOP DISCIPLINE IN YOUR PERSONAL FINANCE

"A man's treatment of money is the most decisive test of his character—how he makes it and how he spends it."
—James Moffatt

As W. Somerset Maugham so sadly pointed out, "The unfortunate thing about this world is that the good habits are much easier to give up than the bad ones." Someone else observed, "Bad habits are like a comfortable bed, easy to get into, but hard to get out of."

We all know that it takes discipline to handle money wisely. Nevertheless, if you develop good money habits, your money will be good to you.

Get a good return on your money

Everyone wants to get a good return on their money. How would you like to make 10% to 20% on your money? Here's an easy way: pay off your credit cards! If you don't have to pay your credit card interest rates of 10% to 20%, it's the same thing as saving or earning that money. Don't be one of the vast numbers of credit card holders who are paying interest on their balances. Be smarter than they are.

Verify your expenses

Open up each bill when it arrives and analyze each bank and credit card statement to check if it's accurate. Put each bill in its own file or envelope.

For your checking account, use check stubs that make a copy of the checks you write. This helps you keep your checkbook balanced because it provides a copy of all the checks you wrote, in case you forget to note it in your records.

Avoid ATMs

Avoid automated teller machines. Sure, ATMs are convenient, but convenience costs. If you use an ATM at a bank branch that isn't your own branch, many banks charge a fee for using that ATM. Some banks have been raising these fees. The fees can add up fast. The cure for ATM dependency is to plan ahead, go to your bank during bank hours, and withdraw the cash you need.

Don't hide your spending behind "saving"

When you buy something, if it is a "want" rather then a "need," it is not a savings, even if you used a coupon or got it on sale. You didn't really "save" money, you spent money. This reminds us of the story of the spouse who proudly returns home from a shopping trip and tells his or her mate how much money all the sales at the store "saved" them. The response from the mate is, "If we saved so much, why do I feel so broke?"

We encourage you to use coupons and shop at sales. Just don't let yourself get carried away by all the spending opportunities.

Earn extra money

To reach your goal of having extra money, you may need to explore beyond your "comfort zone" and look for new ways to make more money.

Weekend or evening jobs can supplement your earnings. You can share your home or apartment with a friend, relative, or tenant and split expenses with them. For extra spending money, you can tell friends and family that you are willing to house sit, pet sit, walk dogs, run errands, or provide other occasional services.

Sleep better at night

There is an old saying, "Make good habits and they will make you." The suggestions in this book work. Pretty soon, your new savings habits will become easier and you will start to see how they make good things happen in your life. Plus, the peace of mind you will gain will help you sleep better at night.

It's not your habits that control you;
it's you who controls your habits.

Chapter 7

OUR BEST MONEY ADVICE: END PROCRASTINATION

"Many people take no care of their money
'til they come nearly to the end of it,
and others do just the same with their time."
—Goethe

A law of physics states, "A body in motion tends to stay in motion; a body at rest tends to stay at rest." When it comes to money, procrastination—doing nothing—can hurt you. You may feel indecisive, not knowing how to start saving. But choosing to do nothing is still a choice with consequences. This choice can cause you to lose out on opportunities that could change the course of your life.

The following suggestions can help you overcome procrastination in your savings program.

Identify your favorite excuses

We all have our favorite excuses for why we can't or won't do the things that we should. For example, we all know we should "eat less and exercise more."

It's a simple concept. Why is it so easy to find good excuses not to do it? We tell ourselves, "I'm too stressed out," "I'm too tired," "I'm too busy," "I'm too upset." We claim, "I don't have enough confidence or energy," "That's just the way I am," or "I can't do this on my own."

Here's the deal: You can pick any excuse. Each excuse works as well as any other. No matter what your reason is, you are using it to stop you from doing what you know you should be doing. You are allowing excuses to paralyze you.

Your excuses may be true and worthy, but it doesn't really matter. The fact is, if you want to increase your savings and improve your life, you need to figure out how to overcome these destructive self-messages.

Think of your "Top Three" favorite excuses for not saving. Write them down and take a look at them. To help you overcome the paralysis that excuses create, here are some ways to get started.

Use automatic savings

Automatic savings is an automatic deduction from your payroll check or your bank account to go into a savings account. You can set aside money weekly or monthly. Once established, the program will work in your favor. Studies show that workers who are on an automatic savings plan are more likely to stick with that plan.

Automatic savings takes only a few simple steps to set up. They work because you never see the money. Some plans can be put into an investment automatically to start earning a return. Study the 401(k) plans and savings plans offered at your place of employment.

Use automatic deposit

You can have your paycheck automatically deposited. This way you can't misplace your paycheck, and your money is available to you faster than if you deposited it in the bank yourself. If you track your bank accounts online, you can see exactly what checks have been deducted and what haven't yet been cleared from your account. Don't forget to check your statement each month for any bank errors.

Use automatic bill paying

Another technique is to pay bills automatically. This is when your bill payments are deducted from your bank account or payroll check and sent directly to the vendor to pay your bills. This prevents you from misplacing your bills, forgetting to pay them, or paying them late. If you've ever paid a bill late, you know about late fees and penalties. With automatic bill paying, your bills are paid on time, every time.

To make automatic bill paying work, be sure you have enough money in your bank account on the day that each bill payment transfer is put through. Otherwise, you will have overdraft charges or checks bouncing. You can protect yourself from overdraft fees by acquiring a line of credit linked to your savings account. Nevertheless, there is no reason to overdraw your account. If you are concerned about exceeding your balance limit, put as much "padding" as you can into your account. But don't spend the padding!

Avoid overdraft fees and late fees

When you have several payments pending, many banks now process the largest check you wrote before they process the smaller checks you wrote. Why? As we mentioned in Chapter 4, banks make lots of money charging overdraft fees. They are more likely to collect those fees and more of them if they deduct the larger check before the smaller amount.

Banks and financial institutions stay in business by making money. To do this, they use your money. To achieve that goal, they need to do several things. They need to acquire as much of your money as possible, keep your money as long as possible, charge you the highest interest rate possible, and pay you the lowest interest rate possible.

On the other hand, the banker at your local bank branch can be very helpful. Go in and create an alliance with him or her. Ask for suggestions about how you can do a better job budgeting, saving and eliminating fees.

You may be able to spread out the payments that are deducted from your account. Ask your creditors to try to change the "due dates" on your bills so that they are not all due at the same time of the month. This will help you manage your finances and prevent overdraft fees and late fees.

**It's not the wishing;
it's the doing.**

Chapter 8

BEWARE OF CREDIT CARD DEBT

"Money often costs too much."
—Ralph Waldo Emerson

Before the days of easy credit for everyone, consumers had to be patient and save until they could afford what they wanted. Patience was a virtue that was respected.

Now that consumers have become dependent on quick, easy credit, they have to dodge credit's one-two punch. Consumers are bruised by the fact that interest payments and fees (1) add up in a short time, and (2) hang around for a long time.

This makes credit-dependent consumers into slaves. "I'm not a slave to debt," you may tell yourself. "I pay my minimum payment on time almost every month." That's exactly what the Money Machine wants you to do! How many times have you resolved to pay more than the minimum payment, but you ended up saying, "I'll wait and do that next month." Meanwhile, you waste today's income paying off the interest burden that you acquired from yesterday's pleasure. The pleasure is in your past, but the burden is in your future.

Credit cards have enormous cost

Credit cards are costing you dearly. Here are some examples:

Example 1: Let's say you want to buy some new technology, a laptop computer, or a big screen television. You decide to incur a $3,000 debt on your credit card that charges you 19.8% interest. If you pay only the minimum required monthly payment, it would take 39 years to pay off the $3,000! (That's assuming that you never mailed a payment late or incurred late fees, which would add to your balance.) Why would it take 39 years to pay it off? The reason is that you would be paying more than $10,000 in interest. Here's the saddest part: You won't be using that laptop or big screen television after 39 years, even though you are still paying for it.

Example 2: Here's a slighting happier scenario. Say you bought something for $2,000 on a credit card that charges 18% interest. According to the *Smart Money Magazine* Sept. 2007 calculation, if you make only minimum monthly payments, it could take 30 years to pay the debt off. In the meantime, you have generously paid your credit card company over time about $4,900 in interest. That means your $2,000 purchase wasn't such a bargain after all. It actually finally cost you $6,900.

Example 3: At this printing, the average household owes about $10,000 on credit cards at an annual rate of 15%, according to the research firm CartTrak.com. This costs about $1,500 a year in interest. If a family invested that interest every year instead and earned 8%, after 40 years they would have an extra $181,700, according to *Smart Money Magazine* Sept. 2007. This is how you can make interest work for you instead of against you.

Some Credit Card Do's

Avoid paying interest and fees

"Low" monthly installment plans are designed to make you feel comfortable and make your creditors rich. It's easy to convince yourself, "Somehow, I will be able to afford the minimum monthly payment." This is dangerous. Instead, make sure that the minimum payment is easy for you and that you will make much larger payments every month in order to avoid paying tons of interest.

We can't tell you often enough: If you can't pay the entire balance, at least pay more than the minimum payment required. Smaller payments now cost more later in deeper and longer debt. It just doesn't make sense to pay the minimum payment. Minimum payments add years and thousands of dollars in interest payments. That's because the interest keeps accruing—and the interest on the interest keeps accruing. The Money Machine has carefully designed the credit card system to keep you in debt for as long as possible.

Credit cards also are designed to slowly consume your money by charging late-payment fees and over-the-limit fees. On some credit cards, if you pay just one day late, you could be charged a late fee. Plus, the credit card company also could increase your interest rate. Over-the-limit-fees can be charged to your account if you spend just one penny past your credit card limit.

Use a plan to eliminate your debt

Wipe your debt column clean. You can do this slowly, but firmly. Take portions of your outstanding debts and pay off a large chunk every month.

Here's how to get started: Make a master chart of all of your debts, who you owe, how much you owe, the minimum monthly payment, the interest rate, and the remaining payments. Add up all the minimum monthly payments.

This is your "monthly payment budget." This amount is the amount you are going to pay *every* month until *all* of your debts are paid off. First, pay off your credit card with the highest interest rate as soon as you can. When that card is paid off, more funds are freed up from your "monthly payment budget" to pay down more of the balance of the other credit cards and eliminate them faster. Keep paying the same amount toward your credit cards until all of the cards are paid off.

As we suggested earlier, consider using some of your savings to pay off credit cards with high interest. If your savings account is earning only half the interest that you are paying for credit cards, this is better use of your money. The key is to: 1) build your savings account back up and, 2) don't use your credit card after it's paid off.

Plan a little reward for yourself when each card is paid off. Then start paying off the next card. When all the cards are paid off, celebrate—and don't use your credit cards except for true emergencies.

Get help if you need it

You may have more debt than you can handle by yourself. More drastic measures may be required, such as negotiation with your creditors for debt relief.

If you are having trouble making your monthly payments, here are some useful websites for credit card debt counseling:

- **www.consumerlaw.org**
- **www.creditguard.org**
- **www.familycredit.org**
  (free booklets on saving)
- **www.myfico.com** (free booklets and a free newsletter about how to save)
- **www.usoba.org** under the consumer link (government advice on choosing the best credit reduction strategy; free newsletter and money saving tips), and
- **www.ftc.gov/bcp/online/pubs/credit/ repair.shtm** (government advice on choosing the best credit counselors)

You can also contact the National Foundation for Credit Counseling at **www.nfcc.org** (800-388-2227).

Pay your credit cards off in full every month

After you learn to control spending and reach your savings goals, you can start using credit cards carefully, charging only the amount that you can pay off fully each month. Surely, you've noticed how interest charges quickly and quietly eat up your income. Now, you will never waste money on interest again.

How will you know what your balance will be each month on each card? Just keep a memo of the date, the amount, and the location of each purchase. That way, when the bills arrive, you will be prepared.

Don't take on more credit

Credit card companies are very aware when you start paying off your cards. It affects their bottom line because now they won't be able to count on you giving them all those interest payments. They want you back into debt. Creditors may start offering you more credit or a higher spending limit, but don't fall for it!

Refuse these offers or you will be pulled down into out-of-control credit again. If they offer you a higher credit limit, refuse it. If they give you credit card checks, shred them. If they send you more credit cards, cut them up.

Report lost or stolen cards right away

Most credit card companies have toll-free numbers and 24-hour service to report lost or stolen credit cards. Keep a copy of the front and back of your credit cards at home, so that this information is readily available. Once you have reported the loss or theft of your card, you usually have no more responsibility for unauthorized charges beyond $50 per credit card.

Acquire credit cards carefully

Some credit card companies offer a "fixed" interest rate. But the "fixed" rate can change without notice. Check your statement every month to see if the interest rate has been increased. If so, call the credit card company to complain. The Federal Reserve is trying to require credit card companies to commit to a specific time period before they can raise the "fixed" interest rate on their cards. However, at the time of publication, this has not been accomplished.

Credit card "enhancements," such as travel discounts, gift certificates and other deals are designed to lure you into obtaining and using credit cards. Face it, once you receive a card, it's hard not to use it and dig yourself deeper in debt.

Buff up your credit rating

One missed payment can lower your credit rating by as much as 100 points. Overdraft charges affect your credit rating, too. As we said before, a poor credit rating can prevent you from buying a home, buying a car, or obtaining a loan. Banks and credit card companies offer lower interest rates to consumers with good credit ratings. A lower interest rate means you save when you need a loan. What is your credit rating, as of today? One way to find out is to go to **www.myfico.com**.

Some Credit Card Don'ts

Don't have more than two cards active

Have a Visa or MasterCard, since some merchants don't accept American Express. An American Express card may be useful if you travel a lot.

Make sure the credit cards you carry have the lowest interest rate available on the market. When possible, switch to a credit card with a lower interest rate. To comparison shop rates, go to **www.cardratings.com**, **www.creditrate.com** and **www.bankrate.com**.

If you have too many credit cards, pay off the extra cards, cut them up and cancel them.

Don't forget to keep your eyes on the calendar

You've heard about "no interest, no payments for a year" credit offers with major purchases. Beware that, at the end of that first year, the interest rate can jump to a very high rate. Unless you are extremely disciplined and know that you will pay the credit debt off early, these deals can cost you lots—not save you lots—of money.

When they say "zero interest" for a year, find out exactly when that year ends and make sure that you have paid off the entire balance long before that date. Otherwise you may have a heart attack when you see your new, high interest rate.

Don't get into an anxiety habit

Overextending your debt creates stress and irritability. This can affect your health and your relationships. You may tell yourself that high levels of debt are "just a part of life." Nevertheless, trying to keep up a wealthy appearance for neighbors, family, and friends can eventually create a heavy burden. We urge you to end the charade. Face up to your feelings of inadequacy. Explore how much you value yourself. Know that the value of each person is so much more than their paycheck or their possessions.

Here is a strategy for those of you who are very disciplined. If you have the cash on hand for the purchase, ask if you can negotiate a discount for cash. If you can't negotiate a discount, you could take the zero interest offer and make the purchase. Then take your cash on hand and invest it in an interest bearing account. Be sure to remember to pay off the debt before the zero interest period ends.

Don't be afraid to ask for help

If you are having trouble controlling your spending, you may benefit from talking to others who have had the same problem. Debtors Anonymous **www. debtorsanonymous.org** uses the very successful 12-Step Program format. Refuse to use your credit card just as an alcoholic refuses to use alcohol. As those in any 12-Step Program know, you can fight your demons only "one day at a time."

Don't use your credit to pay for vices

Gambling, smoking, drinking too much, and illegal drug use are vices that can throw you into out-of-control spending and credit disaster. These personal weaknesses drain tremendous costs from you, both personally and financially.

Gambling causes financial strain, even divorce. Smoking creates health problems that result in medical expenses and a shortened lifespan. Smokers also pay higher premiums on their life insurance, health insurance, auto insurance and property insurance. Alcoholism can slowly destroy one's health, happiness, and family life. The most vicious of all personal demons, illegal drug use, is extremely expensive and potentially deadly.

We all know that these vices are bad for us. Even still, one or more of them may have a steel grip on your life and your finances. If so, do the most simple—but perhaps the most difficult—thing you will ever need to do in your life: admit that you are addicted and that you can't stop by yourself. Then you will find out the good news that you are not alone.

Help is available to reclaim your life, your health and your finances. Click onto **www.nicotine-anonymous.org**, **www.gamblersanonymous.org**, **www.alcoholics-anonymous.org**, **www.na.org** (Narcotics Anonymous), **www.ca.org** (Cocaine Anonymous) and **www.addiction.recov.org** (Illinois Institute for Addiction Recovery). Also, ask your employer or church for referrals to support groups or counselors.

It's not the credit card that is the master;
you are the master.

Chapter 9

SAVING MONEY WITH A BUDGET

"Save a part of your income and begin now,
for the man with a surplus controls circumstances
and the man without a surplus is controlled by circumstances."
—Henry H. Buckley

In order to hang onto your money, you are going to need a budget. A budget helps you control your spending so it doesn't control you. If you have never created a budget before, it is simply a road map that lays out the amount of money you have coming in and gives you guidelines on where you can spend it. Here's how to make a simple budget and stick with it.

Great plans need action to be great

A budget is a plan that won't work unless it is put into action. Once your budget is in place, you can adjust it as needed. Only you know what you really need to include in your budget and what you can eliminate. If your budget is designed for you specifically, you will be able to discipline your spending.

"Most people don't plan to fail, they just fail to plan." Without a plan, we guarantee that your money will disappear and you won't know where it went. Make a plan to keep track of where your money goes throughout the day, the week, the year, and your entire life.

Use a budget guide

To set up your budget, you can use the 27-page budget guide on **www.familycredit.org**. It has worksheets to list creditors, calculate your net worth, your income and expenses, your monthly budget, and your bi-weekly budget.

At **www.teachmeaboutcredit.org** (800-994-3328), you will find a personal budget guide, as well as newsletters that will send you monthly budgeting tips. The Personal Credit Guide points out how you can save thousands of dollars simply by eliminating things like sodas, donuts, morning cappuccino, video rentals and cigarettes. If you are in the habit of buying your lunch on workdays, you may be paying at least $6.00 per day. If you make your lunch at home and bring it to work, you would save $1,500 per year. Not only that, two other things could happen: you could finish your work earlier and you could lose weight!

Be realistic

Everyone has more expenses than they think they do. When you design your budget, be honest with yourself. First add up all of your fixed monthly expenses. Then add in fixed annual expenses including the premiums on all of your insurance policies and property taxes. Make a rough estimate (on the high side) for income taxes, annual physicals, dental cleanings and routine car maintenance. Establish how much you want to spend each year on gifts, travel and home improvement. Don't forget that everyone has unplanned expenses for car repairs, home repairs, dental work, and doctor's visits.

Watch your inflow versus outflow

Now, take a look at your income compared to your expenses. Are you spending beyond your means? If so, you can do one of two things: earn more or spend less.

After you take a realistic look at your situation, set some reachable milestones. Make sure that these goals are realistic, reachable, specific, and based accurately on your true income and outflow of money. Otherwise, you won't stay motivated and reach your goals. Examples of attainable weekly goals are to buy one less cappuccino per week, take your lunch to work once a week, or rent a movie twice a month instead of going to the movie theatre.

Review your assets and debts on a regular basis. Update your budget periodically to stay motivated. Even millionaires need to manage their wealth wisely or they won't remain millionaires.

Use different kinds of money

To master your finances with a budget you need to know about three kinds of money: *fixed* expenses, *flexible* expenses and *discretionary* expenses.

Fixed expenses never change month to month, such as rent or mortgage payments, loan payments, car payments, insurance payments, etc.

Flexible expenses are for necessary items that change in amount month to month, such as groceries, utilities, credit cards charges, household items, clothes, haircuts, etc.

Discretionary expenses are things you can live without, such as dining in restaurants, going to the movie theater or plays, joining clubs and buying books, music and hobby items. It's your daily cappuccino and newspaper. Discretionary items are purchased with what is called *disposable income.*

Know your disposable income

When you cash your paycheck, set aside your savings first. This is called "paying yourself first." Then set aside the money you need to pay your bills and provide for your monthly needs such as food, lodging, health insurance, transportation (bus fare or auto maintenance and insurance).

What is left over is your "disposable income." Save most of this in a special account or envelope for upcoming events, such as travel, entertainment or holidays. You also need a certain amount of "walking around" fun money to use as you wish during the week. Even if your fun money budget is only a few dollars, you can enjoy spending it without guilt.

Make a budget that works

To make a budget that works, first figure out what you spend for the three kinds of expenses listed above. Second, plan to take out the fixed expenses from your income each month as quickly as possible. As we mentioned, you could have online billing that takes it directly from your paycheck. Third, determine a specific amount that you can spend on all the flexible expenses, such as groceries and clothes. Put that amount in cash in a separate envelope for each category. Fourth, at the end of each month, decide what you will be able to spend the next month on discretionary items. Put the cash into a special discretionary envelope and use it for your entertainment desires.

Here's some advice on the psychology of budgeting. If the budget isn't workable or if you deprive yourself too much, you will be tempted to toss the budget in the trash. Make your budget realistic and gradual. If you are patient with yourself, you'll stick with it and see the results.

Have goals

Have a long-term goal to strive toward, even if at times you can only plod along slowly. Long-term goals help keep you from being frustrated by short-term obstacles. If you don't have a vision of a cherished goal—a vacation, a home, comfortable retirement, college—you'll get bogged down in the day-to-day difficulties of life. Remember the old sayings, "You can't hit a homerun unless you step up to the plate," "You can't catch a fish unless you put your line in the water" and "You must be present to win." You can't reach your dreams if you don't try.

What financial goal would make you happier? Being debt-free by the end of the year? Having a certain amount in your savings account? A new car or home? Look at those goals and set them for this year, next year, and the next five years. Now chop those big, annual goals into twelve action steps and establish monthly goals. If you can, slice each of those monthly goals into four weekly action steps. Make sure that your goals are reachable and that you are willing to follow through.

Start with small changes

Start with small, easy behavior changes. You can make your own list, but here are few painless habits to get you headed in the right direction:

1. If you don't shop with a list, start making lists for every store you visit. When you go to that store, bring your list and don't buy anything that is not on the list.
2. When you go to the grocery store with your list, don't go when you're hungry. Have a snack before you go. If you're hungry at the grocery store, you'll buy twice as much stuff. If you bring your children, give them a snack first, too. This saves on whining and tantrums.
3. Try the generic and house brands instead of the brand names. You'll be surprised that they are often identical. Your doctor often prescribes the generic version of a drug, so don't hesitate to try it.

When you build in one of these small changes into your life, start to adopt another change into your life. Small steps will get you there. Just keep moving forward!

Make daily choices that matter

How you spend your money now determines what you will have in the future. Open your mind to opportunities to save money, and they will appear. Act on them and make them a part of your lifestyle. Your actions will either lead to your dreams or destroy you. Choose actions that lead you toward your dreams, not away from them.

Don't think about the temporary struggle necessary to achieve your dreams. Instead, focus on how wonderful it will be to achieve them. Of course, you will have moments of weakness; you may stray off course. The important thing is to get back on track. If you get stuck, whatever you do, don't go backward. Forgive yourself and move on.

Measure your progress through your daily choices. Be glad for even the smallest achievements. Reward yourself in small ways to keep yourself going. Plan a bigger reward for achieving larger milestone victories. But don't let your rewards put you back in debt again.

Use preparation and perspiration

Success requires both preparation (planning) and perspiration (working the plan). If you prepare more, you'll perspire less. The same holds true for your savings and budgeting. A useable, well-designed budget creates a safety net for you. By preparing, you prevent unplanned perspiration.

This phrase hold true for each generation: First plan your work and then work your plan. When you strive, you will thrive.

Study up on it

Read books and magazines. You can read many of these magazines and books free at the public library. See the Suggested Reading list at the back of this book for some suggestions.

Read free online magazines about how to save money. Those magazines are often also available on the magazine racks at grocery stores and bookstores. But why buy them when you can get the information free online or at your local public library?

Here are a few magazine websites to visit:

Good Housekeeping
www.goodhousekeeping.com
(click on the "saving money" tab, then the "budgeting and planning" tab)
Better Homes & Gardens
www.bhg.com
(inside the family and money section)

CNN Money
money.cnn.com
Real Simple
www.realsimple.com
Consumer Reports
www.consumerreports.org

America Saves is a nationwide campaign of more than a thousand non-profit, government, and corporate groups to encourage the financially vulnerable to save and build personal wealth. Go to **www.americasaves. org** to find out more information and suggestions. Also, you can sign up for money-saving tips to be emailed to you daily at **www.dailycents.com**.

Television shows and television news segments offer financial advice and suggestions about consumer products. American Consumer TV **www. americanconsumer.tv** and Real Simple **www.pbs. org/realsimple** on your local public television station are two of many television programs you can watch.

Your newspaper may have a column on how to save. For example, the *Los Angles Times* has a business section with savings tips. You can find out more at the *Los Angeles Time*'s website: **www.latimes.com/ costofliving**. Also, visit libraries and bookstores for books, audio tapes and CDs with financial advice.

As with all advice, carefully analyze financial advice that you hear or read about in the media. Remember, it is designed for the average person, not you specifically.

Ask for advice

When you meet people who are successful at saving and keeping a budget, ask them how they do it. You don't have to "re-invent the wheel."

Ask financial consultants for their suggestions about how you should save and invest your money. Examine their suggestions carefully, and don't rush into anything. Ask lots of questions and listen to the advisors' answers. Do you understand their recommendations? You must decide if their advice is going to help you specifically, not just most people in general.

Even the best advice has its advantages and disadvantages. Sometimes, in their eagerness to promote advantages of a particular financial product or strategy, advisors neglect to fully explain the disadvantages.

One example of lack of communication is "sub-prime teaser-rate" home loans. These loans have a low "teaser" rate at the beginning, in order to help get the buyer into the loan. But the interest rate rises sharply when the loan rate "resets" and the monthly house payment can skyrocket. When home buyers heard the advantages of these loans, they sounded like a great idea. They assumed that they would be able to handle the payments when they increased later. Many homeowners claim, however, that they didn't fully understand the huge potential disadvantages when they signed up for these loans.

It's your responsibility to make sure that the source of any advice you consider—whether from the media, a friend, or advisor—is reputable and qualified to give advice on that topic. No one financial product or strategy is going to fix everything. Test the advice against your "gut" instinct and your research. Does the advice help you reach your goals? (Or do they help the advisor reach his goals instead?) Consider carefully if the advice is practical for your specific circumstances and if you are really comfortable following it.

Be prepared to adapt

"We've always done it this way." These six words are opportunity killers. Change is hard but sometimes it's necessary and often, it's good. Don't be afraid to try new approaches to see if they work for you.

The world will continue to change at an alarming rate, and your life will change along with it. If you think about it, "change" is the only guarantee in life. It is the only thing about which anyone can be sure. We all have to live with the awareness that our current situation could change suddenly at any time—either for the better or for the worse. That's why we always say, "Expect the best, but plan for the worst."

Proactive people plan for any possibility. They are ready to adapt. You can be, too. Build your emergency savings fund now. Then you will be able to be flexible and adjust to the changes that are bound to occur eventually.

Strengthen your character

The choices you make with your money show your true character. Do you feel competitive, greedy, or impatient? Are you unwilling to wait for the things you want?

Take a look at yourself and your financial reality. Build your inner character by doing what you know is right with your finances. This is financial maturity: to accept responsibility for your financial reality and take action to improve it.

It's not what you start with;
it's what you end with.

PART II:

YOUR MONEY & OTHERS

Chapter 10

YOUR MONEY AND YOUR RELATIONSHIPS

*"Whoever originated the cliché that money is the root of all evil
knew hardly anything about the nature of evil
and very little about human beings."*
—Eric Hoffer

Money is not the root of all evil. Money is just a tool to acquire goods and services. It's how people use money that determines whether money is working for good or not.

You've noticed that everyone thinks differently about money. How do the people in your life spend their money? This is a very important question. If you live with someone—a spouse/significant other, a relative, or a roommate—he or she to a certain degree is your financial partner and can help or hurt you financially.

Who is your key financial partner?

If you are married, your spouse is your key financial partner. A divorce would dissolve your legally binding partnership. Even if you don't handle any of your spouse's money, you may still be responsible by law for every financial decision that your partner makes.

How well do you know your spouse/significant other? How well does that person handle his or her money? Does that person desire financial independence like you do? If not, you could be headed for serious, long-term problems both in your finances and in your relationship.

Decide who is the "spender" and the "saver"

Look closely at how your spouse/significant other handles his or her own money, as well as the money you share together. Both of you may say that you want to save money, but one of you may resent the other's desire to spend.

In a relationship, there can be two basic attitudes toward money—the attitude of the spender and the attitude of the saver. The saver desires financial security for both of you. The spender wants a comfortable and pleasurable life for both of you. Which one are you? Which one is your spouse/significant other? Are you working against each other or together?

Don't be afraid to talk about it

Sit down and tell each other why you are either a spender or a saver. Explore how your desire to save or spend is part of your desire to nurture your relationship and care for each other.

Be honest and try to understand each other. Share your inner fears. Acknowledge that each of you is trying to take care of each other in your own way. Since you have formed a financial partnership together, you need to agree on your financial goals and how you can work together to achieve them.

Find common ground, compromise, and meet each other in the middle. There is no question that being responsible and successful with financial matters leads to better and more meaningful relationships. Healthy relationships have enough mutual respect and commitment to adjust to each other's needs and concerns. Talk it out peacefully and thoughtfully. This will help lower some of the emotional walls that have built up between you both.

Don't let money ruin relationships

Studies have shown that one of the greatest causes of divorce is financial stress. Money is one of the most common things for couples to argue about. It's not surprising that disagreements over money cause more than 50% of divorces today.

When you have a conflict with someone about money, multiple things are going on, both with you and the other person. Your motivations about money are in conflict. Try to hear the real meaning behind the words the other person is saying to understand the motivations and fears. If you can "hear" your "inner dialogue" and what is going on inside your partner's head, you can help resolve money conflicts with as little damage as possible.

Everyone is influenced by a combination of money-thinking factors. Your spending and savings motivations are formed by your experiences in childhood, in the work world, and by your expectations about your lifestyle. These various factors can be broken down into five categories, according to the book, *If I Think about Money So Much, Why Can't I Figure It Out?* by Arlene Modica Matthews (see the Suggested Reading list at the end of this book).

Create money harmony in the home

Here are some things to do that will prevent money issues coming between you and your love for each other.

- Invest time in your relationship to show your spouse/significant other that he or she is more important to you than money.
- Read through this book together, chapter by chapter, and circle the things that you are both willing to try.
- Put together a reasonable, realistic budget that you both can support.
- Communicate clearly and reach an agreement about your major purchases and your savings plan.
- Be honest with each other about how and why you make your money decisions. Be sure that your tone is caring, not critical or judgmental.

If you need more help, a skilled professional (a therapist or financial counselor) might be able to help you decide together how to improve your mutual financial situation.

Take a look at the people around you

People tend to start acting like the people around them. Look at the people with whom you and your spouse/significant other associate. Who are your friends and coworkers? Do they spend their money recklessly, foolishly? Or do they know how to save and create value in their lives? Does their behavior influence either of you in any way?

Communicate about purchases

A great way to build money harmony is to honor each other by sticking to your agreed budget. Your definition of a "major" purchase depends on your income. For some couples, a "major" purchase is anything that costs more than $5. For a few couples, even a $5,000 purchase is not a "major" purchase.

Don't make "major" purchases without your partner's approval. If your partner purchased something "behind your back" that you object to, resist the temptation to "pay back" your partner by buying something without joint agreement. Remember, money taken from a joint account or joint credit card belongs to both of you.

If you are on a very tight budget for awhile, it helps if each you of you have an equal amount of fun money for each week. Hold each other accountable for being committed to not spending more than that amount.

Some couples report that they reduce arguments over money by designating their money as either "yours, mine, or ours." That means that they each have their own separate checking account and they share a joint checking account in both of their names. They each have their own separate credit card and they share a credit card in both of their names. As an added benefit, this practice helps establish a healthy individual credit rating for a stay-at-home spouse.

*It's not what you spend together;
it's how you spend together.*

Chapter 11

YOUR MONEY AND YOUR CHILDREN

*"Money won't make you happy
—but everybody wants to find out for themselves."*
—Zig Ziglar

The desire to save is in Sam's and Heidi's DNA—thanks to their parents. They didn't always enjoy learning the lessons their parents taught them, but they learned to appreciate those lessons. Give your children the same gift—the gift of knowing how to save.

Tell your children the truth about money

It's no surprise that children form their ideas about money very early. It's no wonder that they are confused about money. For example, when they see you take money from an ATM, it's natural for them to assume that's how to get money. It's difficult for them to understand the concept of earning an income through employment. They don't see you work many hours and weeks and then receive a paycheck as payment for your labors. Your children will have to learn, as we all had to learn, where money really comes from—from working, saving, and making good investments.

Don't hide your children from "the real world" of money. Gradually introduce them to "the real world." They need to understand that the reason that they can't have everything they want is the same reason that you can't have everything you want. Don't be afraid to say, "I would love to buy that for you, but I'm sorry, I just cannot afford it right now. If you really want it, you can save up for it yourself."

Give your children an allowance

Help your children understand that money needs to be earned, saved, and spent wisely. The best way to learn is by experience. They can start young, so give them a small allowance when they reach kindergarten age. Let them make their own decisions about how to spend their allowance. When they ask you to buy them something special, tell them that they can save their allowance for it or you can give it to them as a birthday or holiday gift. Help them set savings goals, such as to save for a special gift for someone or souvenirs on your family vacation.

Set limits

You will need more money than ever to raise your children. The cost of childcare, schools and college go up all the time. These are costs that you may not be able to control. But you can set limits on your children's spending. When your children are older and they have a cell phone, limit the amount of money you will pay for their bill. For example, they should pay for anything above the base fee. This will teach them to monitor the phone charges they incur.

If you decide to give them a pre-paid credit card or a debit card, set firm limits, such as you will fund the card the same amount on the same day of the month, no exceptions.

Help them to help you

Every generation of parents has discovered the same thing: their children don't really appreciate the sacrifices their parents make for them until they become parents themselves.

Nevertheless, when your children are old enough, they need to understand that they are part of a family and everyone has to pitch in. They can help in the garden, clean their bedrooms and bathrooms, wash their own laundry and help clean up after meals.

Protect your children from temptation

We believe that prepaid credit cards for children generally are a bad idea. It teaches them to depend on credit cards at a very early age. How much better to teach them to be on a cash-and-carry basis and really see their money enter and exit their wallet?

Share this book with your children when they are old enough. Forewarn them about the dangers of debt and hidden costs. Also, many books and programs are available to teach children and teens how to be responsible with their money and become financially literate.

Show your children that it's fun to save

Here's a fun, easy way to show your children how small savings can add up fast: Have everyone in your family toss their loose change into a big "savings jar" at the end of each day. In a few months when the jar is full, help your children take the jar to your bank. Some banks, at no charge, will count your change in a change-counting machine.

Let everyone in the family write down what they think the total amount of change will be. The person who comes closest to the total chooses on which family activity the money will be spent. The family activity could be dining out or a day at an amusement park. The purpose is for everyone to benefit from the time together, since everyone put their change into the jar.

Sam notes that if you spend the family savings jar money on family outings, you are not putting the money away for long-term investment and growth. Heidi counters that memories of family bonding times are important, too.

Make saving a part of everyday life

When your children are young, they can save some of their allowance in their piggy banks and set up lemonade stands, baby-sit and mow lawns. They can learn early to comparison shop for everyday items such as clothes, food, and music.

When they are a little older, your children can open up a savings account at your bank and watch the balance grow. They can mow lawns and organize neighborhood garage sales and get summer jobs at stores or summer camps. To give them incentive to work and put money away in their savings account, you may offer to "match" their funds or reward them when they reach a savings goal. This way, they can experience the satisfaction of selecting and buying larger items they want, such as technology, cars, and auto insurance.

Help them choose a college and a career

Make no mistake, the colleges your children choose will directly affect you and your children's financial situation for years to come in many ways. What are the tuition, room and board, and travel costs? Does the school specialize in their chosen career? While they research these questions, your children can "visit" more colleges remotely by viewing hour-long video tapes of college tours, available at **www.collegiatechoice. com**. Many colleges have Internet tours, too.

Colleges get more expensive every year. Some of the deepest debt is incurred by young people when they are in college. But you don't want your children to be burdened with debt before they even start their professional lives. Help your children understand that they need to help with the expense of their education. Explain to them that their career path will affect their income and standard of living. Student loans take a long time to repay, so they may need to apply for all available scholarships and get a job while going to school. You can get help with college tuition through the Federal Student Financial Aid Information Center **www.studentaid.ed.gov** (800-433-3243). If you have student loans, perhaps you can consolidate them. Visit **www.loanconsolidation.ed.gov**.

Be the role model that they need

Our children are always watching us. We need to do our best to set a good example for them about how to manage money. While it's not always easy, it shows we really care. In more than one way, it's a "priceless" gift that our children will use all their lives.

It's not how much you spend for your children;
it's how much you care for your children.

Chapter 12

GIFT GIVING AND YOUR RELATIONSHIPS

*"Too many people spend money they haven't earned,
to buy things they don't want,
to impress people they don't like."*
—Will Rogers

Gift giving is a big part of our culture. Sometimes, it can be stressful. You may feel insecure if you don't have the right gift for special occasions such as birthdays, showers, weddings and holidays. You may be tempted to spend more than you should, particularly if the person you are buying the gift for is wealthier than you are.

Nevertheless, as in everything in life, you have to hang onto your self-respect and stay within your budget. Here are some ideas on how to save money on gifts.

Give gifts for the right reasons

Keep your reasons for giving pure. Many people place themselves in financial jeopardy by giving lavish gifts beyond what they can afford. Why do they do this? It could be their insecurity that caused them to try to buy acceptance or prestige or to receive forgiveness or love. If you are tempted to do this, take a look at these toxic motivations and what they are doing to your financial future.

Remember the classic Beatles song, "Can't Buy Me Love"? You may be tempted to overspend in an attempt to win someone's affection. Ask yourself some difficult questions: Is this gift really going to make a difference in your relationship? Are you being "used" or taken for granted? Are you giving a "make-up/apology" gift instead of changing the behavior that made the apology necessary in the first place?

Give gifts that will be remembered

Give of yourself. James Russell Lowell said, "Not what we give, but what we share...for the gift without the giver is bare." Instead of spending extra money, spend extra thoughtfulness.

It's not the gift but the thought that goes into the gift that is most appreciated by the recipient. The excellence of a gift lies in its appropriateness. Overly expensive gifts give a false impression and are motivated by insecurity. What you consider to be a generous gift should be generous compared to your income, not compared to the income of the receiver.

To find something unusual and memorable (not necessarily expensive), you can search **www.ebay.com** and **www.froogle.com**. Froogle is Google's product search site.

Give gifts you create yourself

Give of yourself personally by being very creative with the gift, even using your own personal skills to create it. Handmade gifts have so much meaning because you took the time and made the effort. Your creation doesn't have to be perfect. The little handmade cards and gifts children give their parents are treasured, though they are far from perfect. What counts is not the amount of money you spent on a gift, but your personal involvement.

For example, one of Heidi's most treasured gifts from her childhood is the handmade Valentine's Day card that her mother made from leftover fabric, ribbons, and buttons. Heidi enjoys scrap booking and making one-of-a-kind cards.

A gift can be carved, baked, painted, or pasted. You can paint or personalize a pottery item at a Color Me Mine store **www.colormemine.com**, or buy a jewelry-making kit at a store or online and make for a one-of-a-kind necklace, bracelet or earrings.

Give gifts that will be appreciated

A relationship can be damaged when one partner expects the other partner to "read their mind" and to somehow know what they want and to anticipate their needs. Most of us are not good mind readers, so you need to decide first if the gift you want to give is something that the receiver will want.

How do you know what would delight the receiver? Be observant. Listen for their interests and hobbies mentioned in conversations. Ask little questions to find out what they already have. People who know each other well can give more obvious, specific hints.

Give gifts that make a difference

There is an old saying, "If you give someone a fish, you have fed them for a day. But if you teach someone to fish, you have now fed them for the rest of their lives." Your gift can be the gift of mentoring, education, or training. Consider giving the gift of career education to those about whom you care.

Another gift that makes a difference is a good book. The right book read at the right time can literally change someone's life. You can shop for and send a book easily and inexpensively at many bookstores and book websites.

Be practical. When giving gifts and presents, give something that is practical and that will enable the recipient to reach financial independence. Gifts of cash, for those who need it, enable the receiver to use the gift most effectively. First consult with a qualified accountant about any federal or state gift taxes that you might have to pay with a large gift of money.

Use windfalls carefully

A gift of a windfall puts the receiver in a vulnerable position. Remember this whether you are the giver or the receiver. This is an important opportunity that must not be wasted. Make sure that the windfall is used for a long-term goal, such as an education or career advancement.

Windfalls can be prizes, bonuses, inheritances, lottery winnings, and financial gifts in the form of cash, real estate, stocks, or bonds. You may be fortunate enough to receive an unexpected windfall. If so, don't use it foolishly. Use it only for investing long-term in assets that will grow in value, produce income, and increase your wealth.

Consider your windfall as capital. This means you invest it wisely and make it grow. Don't touch the capital, the gift itself. Only use the interest that the gift earns when it's invested wisely. As we explain later, invest in "cows" that give wealth, not "alligators" that consume wealth.

We repeat: Do not spend your capital! Also, this windfall may be subject to taxes. For example, lottery winnings are taxable. Take the taxes off the top and set them aside before you decide what to do with the rest. Remember *TheSmartestWay*™ "wants and needs" question: "What is the best thing that I can do with this windfall?"

Give gifts that accomplish your highest goals

The famous story, "The Gift of the Magi" by O. Henry is about two young lovers at Christmastime. The young husband wants to give his wife the most wonderful gift he can afford, a gold comb for his wife's beautiful long hair. To earn the money, he sells his precious heirloom, the pocket watch that his grandfather had given him. As fate would have it, the wife wants to give him something very special, too. So she cuts off her hair and sells it, to earn the money to buy her husband a chain for his pocket watch. Therefore, the gifts that they each give each other are useless, since he no longer has his prized pocket watch and she no longer has her long hair. The gifts now only represent their devotion to each other.

It's a bittersweet, romantic story, but it's also tragic. To avoid such calamity in your own life, don't allow overpowering emotion to dominate your gift giving. Make sure that your gift will accomplish your highest goals.

Sam points out that the star-crossed lovers in the story would have been much better off if they had communicated with each other. In an ideal world, they could have compared notes and agreed to pool their gift money into saving for a long-term goal such as their dream home, a second honeymoon, or education to help them qualify for a higher-paying job.

Give gifts that are creative

Gift cards are quick and easy. They are more thoughtful than "plain old cash." But they don't say, "I put some thought into this gift. I wanted to give you something special."

The best gifts are creative. Give something selected specifically to please. Give gift cards only when you know that the receivers really would appreciate it. Otherwise, you may always wonder if they ever even used the card.

Give gifts that don't have "issues"

Gift cards have "issues." They can be redeemed only at that particular store, so they are not as practical as cash. (That store, by the way, has been enjoying the use of your money ever since you bought the gift card.)

Gift cards help the stores in every scenario. For example, you may go to the store and buy something for less than the value of the card, and then forget the balance that remains on the card. Gift cards are designed to sit in your wallet and serve as a constant advertisement of that store.

On the other hand, you may go to the store and buy something for a higher price than the value of the card. Therefore, the card spurred you to give the store money that you hadn't intended to give.

Stores know this and they love it. Why do you think gift cards are sold everywhere?

Another problem with gift cards is that some are designed to become worthless over time. A number of years ago, Heidi learned this the hard way at a major discount store (there's one in every town across the land). After she discovered a gift card buried in her desk drawer, she trudged into the store to redeem it. When she made her purchase at the checkout counter, however, she was told that the card had zero value.

The manager made some calls and found out why. The value of the gift card had been systematically devoured by a sentence typed in tiny print on the back of the card. This chain store had adopted a policy called a "monthly non-use fee." Heidi became indignant. Her two sons, who were young at the time, were with her. They were embarrassed that their mom was upset, but they also learned that it's okay to complain about unfairness.

Gifts can be spontaneous and inexpensive

The value of a gift isn't how much money you spent on it. The fact that you went out of your way to be thoughtful and spontaneous is what matters most.

Heidi balances her passion for gift-giving with her need to balance the family budget. Thoughtful but inexpensive gifts can be found at stores such as Stein Mart **www.steinmart.com**, World Market **www.worldmarket.com** and Nordstrom Rack **www.nordstrom.com**. Stores such as 99 Cents Only Store **www.99only.com** and the Dollar Tree stores **www.dollartree.com** have little gift ideas and creative gift bags, wrapping paper, and tissue, too.

Whenever she needs a last-minute gift, Heidi usually can find the perfect item in her spare gift box. When her delighted friends and relatives ask her where she bought their gift, she usually can honestly reply, "I really don't remember!"

Stay rational

Be very careful when it comes to life-changing events that involve deep emotions, such as weddings. Don't let them become a source of friction and anxiety or delay your goal of financial independence because of overspending. The Broadway musical entitled *A Catered Affair* by Harvey Fierstein shows the humor of this situation. Set in the Bronx in 1953, the story is about a couple's dilemma of whether to invest their life savings in a business or spend it all on their only daughter's catered wedding. We all can identify with the characters in the story, even though it took place more than half a century ago.

It's easy to overspend on weddings and wedding gifts, but it's not required. For example, Heidi's most cherished possession is the wedding ring given to her by her husband Bill. The total cost was $300 because the ring's "gem" is a glowing pearl. But the symbolism is priceless for her and she beams when she receives compliments on it.

Keep your sanity during the holidays

Don't wait until the last minute to shop for holiday gifts. Heidi buys a few gifts each month throughout the year when she finds them on sale. That way, she doesn't strain her budget in December or suffer from "post-holiday financial shock." She wraps and labels the gifts and packs everything that needs to be mailed. She mails those gifts right after Thanksgiving to avoid long lines and "rush" shipping charges. Then she can relax and enjoy the true spirit of the holidays.

Sam knows large families, including wealthy ones, that "draw names" at holiday time. This way, you give one nice gift to the name you drew and you get one nice gift from the person who drew your name. Usually there is a maximum price that you are allowed to spend on the gift. Some prefer this instead of buying gifts for every family member. This avoids embarrassment for those who cannot afford gifts for everyone.

Start a holiday fund that you put spare money into each month. At the beginning of the year, calculate your annual gift fund total. For example, if you want to spend $1,200 per year on gifts, save $100 each month.

Keep track of what you spend on gifts, so you don't deplete your fund before the year is over.

Give the gift of words

It's been said that "talk is cheap" and "actions speak louder than words." In many cases, this is true. Nevertheless, words that are a genuine statement of emotion can rich with meaning—if they are the perfect words spoken at the perfect time and given with a perfect heart.

For example, we have a friend who was deeply in love with a very attractive and much sought-after woman. She traveled in high social circles and dated wealthy gentlemen who gave her expensive gifts. The friend won her heart by being attentive to her emotional needs. The poems he wrote for her expressing his love were more treasured and effective in binding them together than any of the material gifts he could have given her.

We've all heard the bitter, sorrowful stories of people who would have done anything in their lives to earn the gift of "I love you" spoken from a parent. While words don't cost a dime, sometimes they are the hardest gift to give. If you need to give a few special words, whether they are of affection, appreciation, or even apology, you may have to sacrifice some pride or resentment. But it's worth the price in order to give a gift that can be treasured for a lifetime.

Give the gift of time

The gift of your time is the most valuable gift of all. Your encouragement, humor, and affection are priceless treasures that will be remembered long after material gifts fade away. If you ever doubt this, just ask the child with a room full of toys but parents with no time to play with them, or the wife with a luxurious home but a husband who is often traveling. "I didn't want more toys—I just wanted you to play with me," says the child. "I didn't want more things—I just wanted you to be with me," says the wife.

For a truly memorable gift, give the gift of making a memory by spending time together. Plan an excursion that has sentimental significance. Carefully plan a surprise that recreates a special moment or recalls an inside joke that you shared together. A gift of a memory that you create by sharing your time, instead of your money, is beyond measure.

It's not how much you spend on a gift;
it's what you give and how you give it.

PART III:

YOUR MONEY & THE WORLD

Chapter 13

WHAT'S BEHIND YOUR OVER-SPENDING

*"You must be in control.
Capital can do nothing without brains to direct it."*
—J. Ogden Armour

Before you can control your spending, you need to know why you buy. If you are feeling insecure, you may go shopping to find something that will help you feel more attractive or more valuable. Sometimes when people are anxious about money, they do the opposite of what they know they should do: they go out and spend even more money.

If you have this problem, you need to start "rewiring" your spending habits. Here are some suggestions.

Don't purchase items you cannot afford

You know in your heart if you can really afford something. You know if a purchase is going to keep you awake worrying at night. Instead, plan for long-term rewards. If you are careful now, eventually you will be able to afford anything you want.

The competitiveness in our materialistic society causes us to make financial decisions that are not in our best interest. Who are you competing with and why? Do they have a higher income level than you? What do you need to prove?

Don't confuse income with self-worth

You are not your paycheck. Your paycheck does not define your worth. (Your spouse's/significant other's paycheck doesn't define your worth or their worth either.) Do not make purchases to help bolster low self-esteem. When money is used as a self-image prop, it leads to financial trouble, which then leads to more negative self-talk. Who is this voice inside your head that says you don't deserve to be happy and financially successful? Refuse to listen, no matter who is saying it.

Don't forget the tortoise and the hare

The story is about competitiveness and pride. The hare, a jack rabbit, wanted to race a turtle. Who won? The turtle, because he was slow but steady and never stopped. The rabbit, however, believed that he could win easily and decided to take a nap during the race.

Sam knows of two brothers. The first one started out with an annual income of about $125,000 per year, and the second one earned $500,000 a year. The one with the lesser income lived comfortably but modestly and traveled on vacations locally. The one with the larger income spent lavishly and toured the world widely.

After forty-five years in their respective careers, which brother ended up a multi-millionaire? The one with the smaller income. He didn't overspend on things that didn't have long-term value. Instead, he invested all he could and made the magic of compound interest work for him. The other brother, although his income was four times greater, now has only 10% of the first brother's net worth.

Don't be afraid to develop a "reputation"

So what if people call you "cheap" or "tight with money"? That's okay. To be a good saver, you can't be concerned about what other people say about you. They need to know that you don't like to waste your money and that you don't like them to waste your money, either.

Your thrifty nature may even make you a legend. Take Sam's "Toothpaste Story," for example. Years ago, Sam hired a new attorney who sometimes appeared overly impressed with the large sums of money necessary to complete their real estate deals. During a high-powered, out-of-town meeting, Sam put a $1,000,000 cashier's check on the table. The meeting took longer than anticipated, so Sam and the attorney had to stay overnight unexpectedly. They found a hotel and went to the hotel gift shop to buy a few toiletries for their overnight stay.

At the checkout counter, the attorney was ready to buy a hair brush, a toothbrush, and toothpaste. Sam was standing in line with a comb, a toothbrush and toothpaste. To make his point about the importance of saving money, Sam told him, "All you need is the toothbrush and a comb, which costs 10% of the price of that hair brush. You can come over to my room and use my toothpaste."

Fifteen years later, the lawyer recounted the incident at a banquet celebrating his success. Apparently, Sam's comment had made a lasting impression on him.

Don't be pressured into lending money

Speaking of social pressure or "peer pressure," here's more good advice: Don't be pressured into lending money. Lending money can ruin your relationships. It happens all the time. Yet, sometimes the pressure is so great that you may be tempted to "give in" and "give a hand-out." We advise you: lend money only if you are willing to turn the loan into a gift.

Remember the rule to "put your own oxygen mask on first"? When it comes to lending money to others, this is a good time to remember this principle. Otherwise, you won't be able to help others in the future. Less than half the loans to family and friends are paid back. Is it okay if you don't get the money back? Are you willing to make your loan into a "gift"? If not, don't give it. To reduce strain on the relationship, make the loan into a gift. Tell the receiver that he or she can pay it back when they are in a position to do so.

You may be asked to help someone by co-signing on a loan. The danger is that if the loan isn't paid off, you are responsible for the balance, whatever it may be. Also, your credit is damaged if the payments are late or in default. If the person were able to handle the loan by themselves, they wouldn't have needed you to co-sign the loan in the first place. So take this into consideration before you take on the liability.

Don't become addicted to Internet shopping

You can become addicted to spending. First you start to crave the emotional "lift" that buying something gives you. Then you come down off that high and feel low because of the guilt and anxiety of spending too much. The cycle continues until it becomes a habit that is difficult to control.

It's very easy to become addicted to Internet shopping. First, you start "window shopping" online to comparison shop. Before you know it, you are a frequent shopper on a multitude of websites. (We all know you can get great deals on **www.ebay.com**, **www.overstock.com** and **www.craigslist.org**, among other such websites.) All this shopping can quickly get out of hand. The point is, you need to be careful not to spend more money and more of your valuable time than you are saving. Make sure that you have a firm handle on your online surfing and shopping so it doesn't become habit forming.

We suggest that you use the Internet to collect information on products and comparison shop only for products that you really need.

Don't become a television shopping addict

If someone is sick in bed or homebound, television shopping is one of their few shopping opportunities. It can also be a social outlet if they call in and talk to the television hosts on the air.

But if you are not bed-bound and you love television shopping channels, you could find yourself spending too much time and money interacting with people and products on the television screen. After all, it's better to shop in person. You can see what you're buying, try it on to make sure it fits and take it home with you.

Don't buy things for instant gratification

Instant gratification is getting something now rather than waiting for the right time to buy it, even when waiting for the right time is far better for your finances.

You may be tempted to buy things to get comfort from them. Remember that the pain of debt lasts much longer than the brief pleasure of getting what you want immediately. Also, when you've waited and saved for something, you appreciate it even more.

Charlie Chaplin once said, "The saddest thing I can imagine is to get used to luxury." Don't buy yourself everything you want when you want it. Instead, whenever the desire strikes to buy things you don't need, set aside the money to pay a larger amount toward your debt or set the amount aside to invest. The financial independence you will achieve will pay you back forever.

Don't confuse your priorities

Much more long-term satisfaction can be gained from personal relationships than from purchases. Do you love people and use things? Or do you love things and use people? Think about it. Woe comes to those who put their professional goals and financial goals ahead of their relationships.

Don't be tempted by envy, pride, or greed.

Envy makes you unhappy because you are coveting another's possessions. As Francis Bacon said, "The covetous man cannot so properly be said to possess wealth, as that wealth may be said to possess him." We all know people who have more than we have. Don't wish that you had what they have. Instead, admire them, be glad for their success, and learn from it.

Pride is feeling superior to others when you earn a higher income or you have more possessions than someone else. There will always be many people who have less than you, so that's nothing to be proud about. Also remember the phrase, "Pride cometh before a fall."

Greed is a powerful temptation in our culture. Fortunately, most of us could survive just fine with much less. Think about how much you consume every day. How big a "footprint" are you leaving on the planet? There is a trend toward thinking about others who are less fortunate and considering the earth's diminishing resources. For examples, check out the website **www. buylesscrap.com**.

Don't think that money can buy everything

Here's a short list of all the things that money cannot buy: health, long life, happiness, self-esteem. Only invested time can help you acquire good taste, intelligence, and good manners. You must earn real love, loyalty, respect, or friendship.

Money also cannot buy control over others. Understand the difference between using money for control purposes versus using it to create freedom. Don't use money to punish by withholding it or to favor one person over the other. Money is to be used to improve your life and the life of those you love.

It's not what you own;
it's who you are.

Chapter 14

SAVING TIPS FOR FOOD AND TRANSPORTATION

"Beware of small expenses;
a small leak will sink a great ship."
—Benjamin Franklin

Saving will soon become an everyday habit for you. With daily practice, soon you'll start getting financially fit. Here are some more ways to save money.

Save on Food

Use coupons

Carve some of the fat from your food budget with coupons. It is estimated that many people save $20 to $30 per week on their groceries by using coupons. That adds up to about $1,000 per year! The time it takes for you to clip coupons is worth it, because it's tax free savings. You can find coupons at **www.dealtech. com**, **www.kroger.com**, **www.couponorganizer. com**, **www.keycodecoupons.com**, and **www. couponcabin.com**. Magazine websites such as

www.goodhousekeeping.com and the Thursday and Sunday editions of the major and local daily newspapers also offer coupons.

Get into the habit of looking for coupons, cutting them out and keeping them organized in a pouch in your car. Of course, keep in mind the concept of "wants versus needs" when using coupons. Just because you have a coupon for something doesn't mean you need to buy it to "save" money. Keep all of your discount and gift cards that you receive in a special file folder. Keep that folder in your car so the coupons are always handy when you shop. Go through the folder occasionally and toss out the coupons that have expired.

Eat better, but eat less

Junk food isn't really food at all. It's just empty calories—calories you don't need. You will be surprised at how much your grocery budget will shrink if you start buying healthier, more nourishing food and less junk food.

Put your food dollars into buying organic dairy products and free-range chicken and meat without hormones. It will taste better, you'll feel better, and you'll be more satisfied. If you don't need to spend extra money on organic fruits and vegetables, wash them thoroughly with a fruit and vegetable cleanser. This helps remove exterior dirt and pesticides.

Eat better and you will eat less because you will feel more satisfied. Not only will your grocery budget shrink, your waistline will too. What's not to like about that?

Rethink the "need" for sodas, coffees

People's dependence on coffee and sodas is a sensitive topic. Many people think they can't function well without their favorite beverage. Unfortunately, most of these drinks are just water filled with some combination of sugar or unhealthy sugar substitute, chemicals, carbonation, flavorings, caffeine, milk, or unhealthy milk substitutes. Besides, they cost too much.

They may taste good, but the bad news is that they drain your wallet and pad your waistline. The good news is that if you eliminate them, you can pad your wallet and slim your waistline.

Liberate yourself from this dependency and learn how to function without these drinks. You may experience a slight headache or feel irritable as your body adjusts to the withdrawal from a mild addiction. If so, cut back gradually, but do cut back. You will improve your health and wealth at the same time.

Avoid fast-food restaurants

Many fast-food restaurants are all about the "fast" and not about the "food." For example, some fast foods are loaded with sodium (salt). If you are addicted to the fast-food habit, break it. It can be costly to your wallet and perhaps your health. Instead, carry handy, healthy snacks with you, string low-fat mozzarella cheese or small bags of mini-carrots, almonds, popcorn, baked crackers, or chips. These taste great with "eat-on-the-run" fruits such as grapes, apples, and bananas.

Make time in your life to eat at home more often. There are many ways to have a nourishing dinner in about the same time you would sit in a drive-through window line. You can buy a pre-roasted whole chicken or packages of pre-cooked chicken pieces to use in salads, burritos, or stews. Put a potato, sweet potato, or healthy microwave dinner in the microwave. You can prepare dinner the night before in a crock pot.

Save on Transportation

Find the right car

The media tells us that driving the "right" car elevates us to higher status. Here's a story about someone who chose the wrong car.

Sam recently was invited out for dinner by an acquaintance. Sam knew that the man was having trouble meeting a monthly office rental of $600 per month. The man was looking for capital to back his real estate projects but never seemed to have any money of his own to invest, even when he earned large commission checks.

To Sam's surprise, he drove up in an $85,000 Mercedes. This explained the problem. The acquaintance was spending too much of his spare funds on a status car, even though he didn't need a status car to impress his clients. A $25,000 car would have been adequate for his needs.

Sam calculated that the difference between buying an $85,000 car and a $25,000 car would have given him $60,000 extra capital to help him develop his projects. Furthermore, investors like Sam tend to be more generous to those who have the discipline to build their cash reserves and thus build their credibility.

Pay cash

Next to your home, your car may be your second-largest purchase. Therefore, you need to buy your cars carefully.

The least expensive way to buy your car is with cash, meaning no loan. You know that, and the dealer knows that. But dealers make a lot of money on financing. Keep this in mind when you shop on the car lots.

You'll get a better price if you don't tell the dealer you intend to pay with cash. Here's why: If you pay cash, the dealer won't receive his commission on the installment plan that he wants to sell you. If the dealer knows he won't be making the commission, he will be more reluctant to negotiate the price and may not give you a bargain.

Whenever you receive an offer from a dealer, tell him you need to think about it. Give him your phone number and then walk off the lot. Often, he soon will phone you with an even better offer. That's because he knows that he has to compete for your business.

If you think you can't afford to pay cash for your car, look for a car you can afford. Heidi and her husband recently bought their Honda Civic with cash. It's a terrific car with high style and low gas mileage. Sam buys his cars with cash, too.

Remember Sam's first car story

Sam bought his first car with cash. In 1950, after his first year at Stanford, Sam took a job as a children's overnight summer camp director in northern Canada. He and two other camp counselors decided that they wanted to go to the nearest town on their days off to get a break from the kids. The problem was that they needed transportation. So they each pitched in $50 and bought a 1936 Dodge sedan for $150.

It was no surprise that the brakes soon wore out. But the young men couldn't afford new brakes. Instead, they discovered that they could stop the car by putting it into second gear and coasting to a stop. At the end of the summer, they left the car at the camp. Sam wonders if it's still there. Now, when he fills his car with a tank of gas, he can honestly say that it costs him more than what he paid for his first car.

Be careful with installment plans

If you can't pay with cash, you'll have to buy with a loan. When you are out on the dealer's lot or in the showroom, you will be approached by convincing, enthusiastic salespeople. Before you know it, you'll be looking at attractive cars that are beyond your budget.

An installment plan offer may seem like "free money" and convince you to buy a more expensive car. But beware: an installment plan costs you enormously in interest payments. That's why you need to first compare the dealer's loan offer with your credit union's or bank's loan offer. Dealers often make more on the financing arrangement than they do on the car, so they will be very eager for you to finance with them. If possible, get a pre-approved loan from your credit union or bank before you even go shopping.

Make the largest down payment you can afford. Don't choose the longest payment plan, even though your monthly minimum payment would be lower. The longer you spend paying the loan back, the more interest you are going to pay. Ask the dealer to calculate what the interest will be on the various payment options. You'll be surprised how fast the interest adds up. Longer payment plans often carry higher interest rates as well.

In economic downturns, installments can become harder to pay. They also put you at risk. By that, we mean that if you find that for whatever reason, you cannot make the payments, the dealer may repossess your car. To lose your car through repossession is a major blow to your pride, your mobility, and lifestyle. It also inflicts permanent trauma to your credit rating.

Before you buy, remember that cars, boats, and recreational vehicles cannot be repossessed if you pay for them in cash.

Do your homework

If you do your research, you will find a good car that you can afford. There are dozens of manufacturers and models and dealerships from which to choose. They all are hoping for your business.

Before buying a car, adopt *TheSmartestWay*™ philosophy. Ask yourself, Is this the car going to help me save money? What can I really afford? How much will my auto insurance premiums increase? What am I willing to give up to be able to afford this car? What kind of car and size of car do I really need?

Now, do your homework. The Internet is a good place to start. Search online at **www.kbb.com** (The Official Kelly Blue Book), **www.autosite.com**, **www.carfax.com**, **www.carwizard.com**, **www.consumerreports.com**.

In your research, look at gas mileage. If your car gets lousy gas mileage, that adds to the price of the car. To compute your total cost each month for your car, don't just look at the monthly payment and interest cost (if you have to finance it). Also add in the average monthly cost of gas, insurance, repairs and maintenance. Remember that a more economical car will save you significantly on each of these expenses.

You can find hybrid cars that use less gasoline at **www.allhybridvehicles.info**, including the hybrid versions of Honda Civic and Accord, Chevy Malibu, cars by Lexus, Nissan and Saturn, as well as the Toyota models: Prius, Camry, Highlander and others. With the price of gas these days, hybrids aren't just for environmentalists anymore.

Comparison shop

Once you have decided what types, brands, models, and years of cars you want to consider, start comparison shopping.

Whatever car you decide to buy, first compare the online prices to the dealer prices. The sticker price on the window is the highest price that the manufacturer recommends. You want to pay much less. Prices will vary from dealership to dealership. So will customer service.

Buy your cars like Sam buys cars

Don't hesitate to use one dealer against the other. They are used to it. They expect it. They just hope that perhaps you will decide to finally make your purchase with them.

Recently when Sam bought a car, the local dealer quoted him a price that Sam thought was too high. He comparison shopped at another dealership that had the largest inventory of that make in the state. That dealer was located some distance away, but the trip was worth it. The second dealer offered Sam a much better price.

Sam returned to his local dealer with the lower price, and his local dealer matched it. The reason he wanted to finally buy from the local dealer was for the convenience. For the model of car he bought, he would get better service and more privileges at the dealership where he bought the car. Once again, it pays to comparison shop and use one price against the other.

Know the dealer's cost

When buying a car, Sam always determines the dealer's actual cost on all the accessories and add-ons. Accessories can include floor mats, chrome strips, specialty hub caps, GPS systems and a myriad of other add-ons. The price of some auto accessories can include as much as 40% in dealer profit. You can determine the actual cost from the American Auto Club **www.aaa.com**, the Official Kelly Blue Book **www.kbb.com**, and Edmund's **www.edmunds.com**. Get negotiating tips and quotes from websites such as **www.autobytl.com**, **www.autoweb.com**, **www. intellichoice.com**, **www.carpoint.com**, **www. carbargains.com**, and **www.carmax.com**.

Negotiate to have the accessories added to the car at the time of purchase at cost. This can save you lots of money. Also, some accessories can be acquired at no cost when you negotiate the price, since the expense to the dealer may be minimal. Do some research at **www.dontgettakeneverytime.com** and **www. nhtsa.dot.gov/cars/problems** (the National Highway Traffic Safety Administration).

Avoid the leasing trap

Leasing a car is the most expensive way to own a car. It seldom makes good financial sense. It has been said that, "Leasing a car is a poor man's way to look rich." Nevertheless, you will feel a lot of pressure from your friends and from the dealers to lease a new "status" car. Almost half of all car purchases these days are leases. The dealers, of course, are very happy about this because they benefit from handling the financing.

If you lease a car, you make a down payment and monthly payments. These are lower than if you were buying the car. It's like renting a home with a "lease with option to buy" type contract. The longer the lease, the lower your monthly payment, but the higher the interest you'll pay. Not only will you pay enormous interest payments during the lease, you get hit at the end of the lease, too.

As in renting an apartment versus owning a home, it's usually better to own than to rent (lease), because the owner of the property has the upper hand. For example, if you decide to buy the car at the end of the lease period, you may find yourself paying more money than you should, since your car has already lost much of its value. If you don't purchase the car and you decide to return it, the car must be in the same condition as when you bought it, normal wear and tear excepted. You must pay the dealer's costs for fixing any damage to the car. Also, if you exceeded the mileage limit, you pay his fees for that, too.

If you choose to pay off your lease early, you may have to pay an "early termination" penalty. Lenders usually require an early termination fee because you are denying them the interest fees they were expecting to receive from you.

In addition, leases are very difficult to understand. Make sure the dealer explains everything to you in detail and prints out all explanations of the policy. Almost everything is negotiable, so negotiate.

Buy a used car, and buy it with cash

A new car depreciates by at least 20% the minute you drive it off the dealer lot. This adds up to thousands of dollars! Twenty percent of $20,000 is $4,000. We ask you, is a couple weeks of "new car smell" really worth $4,000?

The best cars to buy are certified, pre-owned cars. The best way to buy these cars is with cash. That's how Heidi's parents bought their cars; that's how she buys her cars. Even Sam buys used cars when he feels it makes sense, and he always pays cash.

There are many good, certified, pre-owned cars out there from which to choose. If you shop carefully, you can find a well-maintained used car for half what a new one would cost. Before you buy any car, get the car's vehicle identification number (VIN) and type it into **www.carfax.com**. You will receive a vehicle history report of any prior accidents or flood damage.

If you drive your car for a long time and get the value from it, eventually it may not be worth very much. You may want to sell it back to a dealer or trade it in. Before you decide, check with several dealers, as their offers will vary. If the car is valued at less than $500, you might be better off to give it to charity for a tax deduction.

Don't go "upside down"

You are "upside down" on a possession if you owe more in payments than the item is now worth. Here's how to find out if you are "upside down" on your car payment: Determine what you still owe on your car (including interest that you will have to pay). Then determine approximately what you could sell you car for today. Which is the higher number? Do you owe more than your car is worth?

Save on gas

The price of gas these days has captured everyone's attention. But you can find gas stations that have lower prices, sometimes 20 to 30 cents a gallon less. To make it worthwhile, fill up whenever you pass a station with a lower price. At the gas stations along Sam's commute to his office (approximately five miles), there is a 10¢ to 40¢ difference in the price for the same grade of gas, depending on the location of the station and the brand of gasoline. If you use a tank every two weeks, this can amount to several hundred dollars in savings per year.

Here are some ways to save on gas:

1. Comparison shop for gas. Prices vary at different gas stations and on different days.
2. Drive at an even pace. Break the habit of fast starts and sharp braking.
3. Use cruise control wherever appropriate.
4. Combine your errands so you can do most of them in one trip or in one location.
5. Drive a fuel-efficient car. Not all of them are small.
6. If you choose a larger car for safety, choose one that is fuel efficient.
7. Walk or ride a bike for short trips.
8. Telecommute as often as you can.
9. Try to get flex-time so that you commute during non-peak hours.
10. Remove unnecessary items from your trunk. Extra weight uses more gas.
11. Keep your car in good condition and tuned up. Change the oil and keep your tires properly inflated. A well-maintained car gets better gas mileage.
12. Use light rail, buses and other forms of public transportation, which can be more convenient than you realize.
13. Car pool or van pool to work. Ask your employer to help. Some cities provide subsidies.
14. Coordinate car pools for your kids to go to school and set up schedules with other parents for after-school events.
15. If you have two cars, use the car that is more fuel efficient for daily commuting to school or work and for longer drives.

16. Sometimes, renting a car for long trips makes sense, as you avoid putting the wear and tear on your car. Enterprise Rent-a-Car **www. enterprise.com** provides discount coupons if you sign up with them.
17. Drive within the speed limit. Driving at higher speeds uses more gasoline.
18. If you are tempted to drive fast because you are stressed out by traffic, chill out! Get some interesting CDs or audio tapes to listen to in the car. Thousands of books-on-tape are available from audio book rental clubs on dozens of different topics. Take a look at the selection at **www.onthegobooks.com**, **www. simplyaudiobooks.com**, or **www.audible. com**. Motivational tapes, learning-a-language tapes and MP3 downloads of trainings and radio shows are other options. Also, you can check out audio books for free from your library.

It's not what you drive;
it's what you pay for what you drive.

Chapter 15

SAVING TIPS FOR UTILITIES AND MEDICAL NEEDS

"Money isn't everything
–but it ranks right up there with oxygen."
—Rita Davenport

Utilities and medical needs take up more and more of our income. Be a watchful consumer and you'll save money.

Save on Utilities

Lower utility bills

Insulate your home to prevent hot and cool air from entering your home. Lower your home's temperature in the colder months when you are away or sleeping. Ask your gas and electric provider for a free "energy survey" inspection in your house to find ways to lower your energy bills. They may provide an optional "budget billing" to balance out your heating bills. For your television service, buy just the basic plan for your cable channels. If your water or gas bill rises unexpectedly, check to see if you have a broken or leaking gas line or water pipe.

Save on phone bills

For long-distance calls, you can save by using discount phone cards from discount stores such as Wal-Mart **(www.walmart.com)** and 99 Cents Only stores **www.99only.com.**

Heidi has used one long-distance prefix code for years. It bills all domestic long-distance calls at five cents per minute. She dials the code number 1010811 before she dials the number she's calling. To try it out, dial that code number in front of the long-distance number you are calling. Note the length of the call. Then check your phone bill for the charge.

You can even switch from making nationwide calls from traditional phone service to Internet phone service. If you have a computer and you can be connected to the Internet continually, this may be a way for you to save money. The cost of new technology is dropping all the time. Find the best deals.

Save on cell phone bills

If you use your cell phone continually, you may consider canceling the landline telephone in your home. But be sure to watch your charges and fees on your cell phone, especially when you are out of town. Roaming charges can be very costly.

Talk to your cell phone carrier about analyzing your calling patterns. You may be able to switch to a less expensive plan.

Cell phone contracts can be tricky. Be sure to ask lots of questions and read the fine print for upgrade fees and cancellation fees. Comparison shop with all available carriers and ask each carrier why you should pick them instead of their competitors. When you get your bill, inspect it for charges you didn't order, fees you don't understand, and penalties for exceeding allotted minutes. Also beware of cell phone insurance policies. The replacement cell phone you receive through the insurance coverage may be used or refurbished.

Complain effectively as a consumer

Whenever you have a complaint about a utility service or any product, first prepare your case. Write down the facts of your complaint. What went wrong? What would fix the problem for you? What will you accept from the company in exchange for ending your complaint?

When you talk to a representative, make a note of the date, the time, and the person's name, title, and phone number. Write down what they said and repeat it back to them to make sure they agree with what you wrote. Then ask to talk to their supervisor. Be friendly but firm. If you get a "no," ask to talk to the next person in charge. Keep going up the chain of command until you get an answer you can accept.

They want you to get frustrated with the obstacles and delays and to give up. We've all heard the phrase, "the squeaky wheel gets the grease." It's true. Persistence helps.

If this doesn't work, you can contact **www. consumeraction.gov** or your local Better Business Bureau office. There are consumer complaint websites that create public relations embarrassment, such as **www. ripoffreport.com** and **www.consumeraffairs.com**.

If you need to get out of your cell phone contract, you may be able to find someone to take it over for you, perhaps on websites such as **www.cellswapper. com** and **www.celltradeusa.com**. Also, you may be

able to get out of your contract if there has been a
price change affecting your plan.

Save on Medical Needs

Try generic and over-the-counter drugs

Medicine is not necessarily a "you get what you pay
for" situation. Many generic versions seem to work as
well as their more expensive counterparts.

Check with your health insurance provider

Before you get your annual physical checkups, bi-
annual dental cleanings, etc., call your health insurance
provider. They can tell you if the visit will be covered by
your policy. If you receive a serious diagnosis, ask your
health insurance provider to assign a "case manager"
to you. That manager can help you qualify for additional
services.

Carry your health insurance card at all times

This will help you get speedy care and assure
that you are billed properly in case you ever need
emergency services. If at all possible, ask the hospital
or the doctor's staff to call your health insurance
provider to receive pre-approval of your treatment.

Be forewarned that some health insurance providers
won't insure services provided at certain hospitals or
doctors' offices. This would be the case if the hospital
or doctor doesn't have a contract to get paid by the
provider. This happened to Heidi. Her two sons' health
insurance plan is no longer accepted by the hospital
near their home.

Payment for any treatment you receive is ultimately
your responsibility. If the treatment you receive isn't

covered by your insurance, you will have to pay for the treatment yourself.

Be an active participant in your health care

Every time you visit the doctor, bring a list of questions. Write down the answers. When a doctor orders a test or procedure, ask if it is really necessary. If so, why? If it's a redo, why does it need to be repeated? Could repeats be dangerous? You deserve the answers to these questions. It's your body and your wallet—not the doctor's!

Stay on top of the details

We hope that you never have to enter a hospital as a patient. If you do, one of the best things you can do is get a notepad and write down as much as you can. If you are in no condition, physically or emotionally, to take notes, ask a friend or family member to keep track of things for you.

When you check in, you may be required to give the staff your personal items, such as your wallet and jewelry. List all your personal items and their value on your notepad. Ask for and keep your receipt. This will help make sure that you get everything returned to you.

Write down the names of the tests you receive. Keep a list of the location and duration of any pain and symptoms you may feel. When doctors come in to your room to check on your condition, try to write down their name and what they told you about your condition and what they advise you to do.

Get a patient's representative at the hospital

A patient's representative is an advocate provided for you at some hospitals. Ask to be introduced to him or her as soon as possible. Get all of their available contact information. He or she should be able to pass along your complaints or suggestions to the proper authorities. This can save you money by eliminating miscommunication and perhaps shortening your stay at the hospital.

Review your bill

Before you check out of the hospital, you may receive a hospital bill. Study it carefully. Be sure to get a fully itemized version, even though it may be pages long. Phone the billing office of the hospital to request an explanation of charges that don't make sense or that could be errors. Dispute any charges that don't coordinate with your records. If you have a dispute, call your insurance provider. If your employer has an insurance department, they may be able to help, too. Don't sign off on a bill until you are satisfied.

Be sure to save all receipts, billing, and documentation for your tax preparer or accountant. This will help you get all allowed deductions for medical expenses.

Get the best

Not all doctors are created equal. Get the best medical care that you can afford. It could be a matter of life and death. If you feel that one doctor isn't listening to you or doesn't really understand your symptoms, ask to see another doctor. If you're not satisfied with the second doctor, go to another. Even HMO insurance plans allow for a "second opinion."

This is what Heidi's friend did recently. The first three doctors each gave her a different medicine, each for a different illness. But she still didn't know what was making her sick. Finally, the fourth doctor took a test that uncovered the problem. Fortunately,

Heidi's friend had followed her "gut" instinct and kept searching for the cause of her illness. Otherwise, she would have been taking medicines that would only make her condition worse.

Please don't settle for a misdiagnosis. You have to know what your problem is before you can treat it. Treating the wrong problem only makes you sicker.

Save the best way on medical needs

The best way to save on medical needs is to not need them in the first place. Get in good health and stay in good health with a wholesome diet, lots of exercise, and no addictions. Create as much love and laughter in your life as you can.

We know that making time for exercise is hard for most people. We try to practice what we preach. Sam has a personal trainer who comes to his house several times a week. Other days, he spends time on his treadmill. Heidi and her husband visit their local YMCA several mornings per week and take walks together.

To start the exercise routine that works best for you, visit a number of local fitness clubs and compare their prices and amenities. Depending on where you live, YMCAs, YWCAs, and other clubs can provide athletic facilities at reasonable rates.

Wherever and however you get your exercise, get out there and get going!

It's not your wealth;
it's your health.

Chapter 16

SAVING TIPS FOR TRAVEL AND ENTERTAINMENT

"It is not so hard to earn money as to spend it well."
—Spurgeon

Travel and entertainment make life worthwhile. You can't eliminate them from your life. Instead, find new, less expensive ways to enjoy trips with your loved ones and fun time with your friends.

Save on Travel

Know why you are taking the vacation

The quality of a vacation is not based on how much money you spend. What counts most is the closeness, harmony, and happy memories that the trip creates. Approach your vacation from the philosophy of *TheSmartestWay*™. Ask yourself, "What would enrich my relationship with my loved ones? What is the best way to spend quality time together?"

When you plan a trip with your loved ones, schedule plenty of "bonding time." If you have younger children, this is what they will remember most. They won't remember how much money you spent on an expensive dinner as much as they will remember that on the way to dinner, you stopped the car by the beach and suggested that you all sit on the sand together to watch the sunset.

One of the best vacations in Heidi's childhood started with a disaster. The family station wagon broke down in a little town on the way to their destination. The repairs took several days, but the auto insurance company paid for the nicest hotel in town. To her delight, the hotel had a swimming pool. The relaxed afternoons playing in the pool together became a family memory.

Know where to go

Where you go determines how much you will spend. Have you really explored all of the interesting things to do in your city or your state? If you don't have a budget for gas or airline tickets, you can still have a memorable vacation. Reserve a nice room at the best hotel in your town or the nearest city. Tour the art museums, eat at the top restaurants, and attend a concert. You can even have friends join you for your cultural, elegant, but lower-cost "getaway." You could have spent twice the time and money traveling to another state or country, but you may have just as much fun in your own city.

Your local automobile club, chamber of commerce, and community tourism offices can suggest nearby excursions. Check with your state tourism office to find all the activities and destinations in your state. Most of these offices have websites, too.

If you want more room to spread out, consider hotels with suites such as **www.embassysuites.com**, **www.residenceinn.com**, **www.homesteadhotels.**

com, www.amerisuites.com and www.radisson. com.

If hotels are out of your budget, there are plenty of day-trips in your area to explore, including the national and state parks. Kids love simple times such as hiking, building a campfire, and roasting marshmallows with their family.

Know how to get a bargain

When you travel, you will spend extra money, so plan ahead and stretch your travel budget. Comparison shop on the Internet. Sites such as Trip Advisor www. tripadvisor.com save time. Just plug in the location you are seeking and up pops everything on that location from the other discount travel sites. Visit www.orbitz. com, www.expedia.com, www.travelocity.com, www.hotels.com, and www.priceline.com for bargains on rental cars.

With rental cars, you may not need to buy insurance. Call your own auto insurance provider to find out if your insurance protects you in the case of an accident while driving a rental car. Find out if your coverage is for a limited number of days traveling or if is limited to just the United States.

Membership with automobile and RV associations may entitle you to a free magazine about traveling. For example, members of AAA of California www.aaa-calif.com receive *Westways* Magazine, which contains suggestions for California drivers on how to save while traveling.

Know how to negotiate with hotels

When you book your hotel, always ask, "Can I get a better rate? Can I get an upgrade at no charge?" Often, the hotel reservation operator will say that they cannot commit to an upgrade but they will put in a request. When you check into the hotel, be sure to ask, "Can my room be upgraded at no extra charge?" They may put you in a room on the executive suite level. Some hotels have executive level lounges that provide computers, printers, beverages, and appetizers.

Recently, Heidi made a hotel reservation. She asked if she could get a discount or upgrade because she is an AAA member. Hotels often shave a few dollars off the price of the room if you are an AAA member. To her delight, the hotel offered her a junior suite on the executive level, free valet parking and breakfast.

Early check-in and late check-out are no-cost upgrades that extend your hotel-stay options. Many guest rooms are ready to be occupied by 10:00 a.m. Some hotels extend the required checkout time to 4:00 p.m. This can allow for a nice nap after sightseeing and lunch. As we like to remind you, it never hurts to ask.

Know where your wallet is

Watch for pickpockets and credit card thieves. When you're traveling, you're distracted by finding your way around, keeping track of your luggage, and having fun with your loved ones. When you are in an unfamiliar environment, it's easy to lose track of your wallet or credit cards. Thieves know this.

Some people wear a "dummy wallet" with $20 in it. They keep their real wallet in a special travel pouch or their sock. If you wear a fanny-pack, find one that has a hidden clip-hook and steel-enforced webbing so that the fanny pack can't be easily unclipped or cut off your waist by a thief.

Whenever you use your credit card, always check three things: 1) you are charged for the right amount, 2) you get your card back, and 3) the card you get back is actually yours. As for bank traveler's checks, they may seem like a good idea. However, many people neglect to redeem leftover traveler's checks after the trip is finished. This is not productive use of their money.

Know how to check into the hotel

Ask questions when you hand over your credit card as you check into a hotel. Many major hotels put a "hold" on a certain amount of funds on your credit card. Ask what the "hold" amount is and when it will be billed. You may even be charged for one or more nights when you make your reservation. Each hotel has a different policy. The "hold" shouldn't affect your ability to charge on the card unless you're up against your credit limit. Plan ahead so that your credit card doesn't suddenly max out.

Don't use a debit card to check into a hotel. At least one major hotel chain actually withdraws funds from your checking account as soon as you check in. The hotel takes out the daily rate for the number of days you are planning to stay. For example, if it's a four-day stay at $75 per day, $300 will be taken out of your checking account as soon as you check into the hotel! The $75 per day deduction is for "estimated average incidental charges" you might incur, such as snacks and drinks from your room's mini-bar, dining at the hotel restaurants, the hotel's dry cleaning service, etc.

If you don't spend $75 per day in incidentals at the hotel each day, you will get a refund. Here's the kicker: the refund isn't credited back to your checking account until 72 hours after you check out of the hotel. Some hotel guests have found that the incidentals charges were not paid back until over a week after they check out of the hotel.

If you absolutely must use a debit card at a hotel, make sure it contains sufficient funds so the daily charges don't empty your account or cause you to bounce checks. After your trip, call your bank to make sure that your reimbursement of the daily charges was returned to your checking account.

The best way to find out what is going on at the hotel is to ask. The clerk may not be able to tell you, so ask a manager. Ask until you get a clear answer.

It's your money, but when you give them your debit card, they can take whatever they want, whenever they want it and return it whenever they want.

Know how to check out of the hotel

When you check out of the hotel, examine your bill before you agree to it. The local taxes, bed taxes, and government taxes may take your breath away. Then there are parking fees, movie and video game rentals, room service, and phone calls. Make sure that you agree to all the charges listed. Have a manager remove the errors from your bill and give you a corrected bill for your records. Also, if there were any problems, such as no warm water in the morning for showering, tell the manager about it. You may receive a free night's stay.

Know how to watch for hidden charges

Unfortunately, hotels and other travel services know how to slip their fingers into your wallet as well. Fortunately, there are ways to avoid having your wallet cleaned out unnecessarily. Here are a few things to watch out for.

Many hotels have a small refrigerator filled with drinks and snacks in the room. It is sometimes called a mini-bar. When you check into the room, the clerk will ask you if you would like a mini-bar key. If you refuse to take the key, you won't be tempted to snack. The refreshments are extremely overpriced, so a few snacks can add up fast.

Some hotels display the snacks and drinks on a tray in the room. Just because they aren't in a locked mini-bar doesn't mean they are free. The snack tray may be plugged into an electrical socket. If you remove those tasty treats from the tray to prevent you or your children from being tempted, beware. A sensor may automatically bill your room if the items are removed for the tray for more than a few seconds. What a surprise when you see the charges on your bill!

Save on Entertainment

Look for new ways to have fun

"A fool and his money are soon parted," can be put another way: "A fool and his money are soon partying." It's time to trim your entertainment budget. Here are ways to be money-wise and still have fun.

Do you miss those nights of going out for dinner? Make something special to eat at home. It may taste even better than a restaurant dish and will surely cost less. Don't want to spend money on cookbooks? The Internet is full of recipes for every skill level and every ingredient.

When you do go to a restaurant to eat, here are ways to save: split your dinner. Most restaurants will give you extra plates so you can share your salad, entrée and dessert. If you still have food left over, ask for a "doggy bag" so you can take it home. Restaurant leftovers are usually very tasty the next day. The whole family can eat economically at family style buffet restaurants. For locations near you, visit **www.buffets.com**, **www.souplantation.com** and search on the Internet under "all-you-can-eat restaurants."

Do you miss going to the movies? You can check out DVDs and VHS videos for free at the library. You can buy them for a dollar or two at thrift stores. If you are sick at home or have lots of time to watch movies, give Netflix **www.netflix.com** a try. You can have a two-week trial membership for free and access to almost every movie ever made.

If you do go to the movies, don't buy those high-priced snacks at the theater. We ask you: how can a bucket of popcorn really be worth $7? It can't. Heidi and her husband stock up on their favorite "movie candy" whenever they visit the 99 Cent Store **www.99only. com**. If your theater allows it, simply carry in a can of soda and a box of candy in your purse or pocket. What you save in snacks can be used toward another evening at the movies, so everyone wins.

Look for something different to do

In the mood for some intellectual or cultural stimulation? When was the last time you visited your local museums? Your local library and your local community have free seminars, classes, and historic and world tour seminars. There are usually free concerts in the park where you can take a picnic and make a day of it with your friends.

You may love golf or other expensive activities, but there are so many other hobbies and sports from which to choose. Branch out and try something new. For example, your local community college catalog will tantalize you with inexpensive classes to broaden your interests and your skills, as well as provide the opportunity to make new friends.

Throw fun, creative parties

People love to attend parties with a theme, such as toga, luau, western, disco, fifties, etc. Co-ed pajama parties are lots of laughs, because everyone wears their PJs and plays Charades, Monopoly, Twister, or other old-fashioned kid games. Spa parties are an inexpensive alternative to "girls' night out." Everyone dresses in robes and slippers. A home skin-care line demonstrator gives each guest a facial, while the other guests give each other manicures and pedicures.

Instead of a theme, your party can have a purpose, such as wishing someone a good vacation (a bon voyage party), witnessing wedding vows re-confirmation, or even celebrating a return to health at a recovery party. Heidi has a friend who throws a party every year to celebrate her anniversary of yet another year of being free from breast cancer.

Ask for what you want

Restaurants can be helpful when planning a party. It never hurts to ask. One of Heidi's favorite Los Angeles restaurants allows her to hold a party very economically. The elegant, private dining room serves 8–20 and can be reserved for two hours. All that's required is a commitment of a minimum of eight guests who spend a minimum of $20 per guest.

Don't be too proud to "potluck"

Heidi's favorite method of home entertaining is "potluck." It saves so much time, money, and hassle for the hostess. Each guest brings something—a salad, some meat to grill, bread, beverages or dessert—so you usually have enough, even if you don't know how many guests will arrive. Just to be safe, you can provide the main course of barbeque, or a big pot of stew, chili, or spaghetti. There can be a theme, such as Mexican or Italian. Or you can make it totally random and see what delicious surprises arrive.

Guests don't mind contributing food and many enjoy sharing their favorite dishes. The menu becomes eclectic, fun, and a topic of conversation. Everyone pitches in. Those who don't like to cook or don't have time can bring beverages or a store-made dessert or breads.

If you have a big family or lots of friends who like to get together frequently, how about starting a tradition of a regular potluck brunch or dinner? You could set the date as the second Sunday of every month, alternating at each other's homes. To spice up the conversation, you could ask everyone to bring a "share time" item, like when you were in elementary school. The item could be as varied as poem to read, a piece of music, or a photograph.

Save on invitations

The cost of professionally printed invitations goes up all the time. Elaborate, expensive invitations are so popular that sometimes hosts spend as much on the invitations as they do on the entire event. Unfortunately, few people save invitations. Most of them end up in the wastepaper basket when the event is over. Why not spend the money instead on something more memorable, such as entertainment at the event or the table gift favors?

Invitations can be creative, memorable and inexpensive. If most of your guests use email, invite them online with Evite **www.evite.com**. Evite has hundreds of creative, classy, pre-designed email invitations for every possible occasion. You can send an unlimited number of invitations entirely free.

For paper invitations, visit craft stores such as Michaels **www.michaels.com**, scrap-booking stores, and the Internet for ideas about creative do-it-yourself handmade invitations. Home color printers can print attractive, customized invitations. Maybe a friend can help you design them. Wedding invitation kits include matching satin-trimmed cards, sheer velum sheets, envelopes and small, matching RSVP cards and envelopes to be inserted into the invitation. These can be printed on a home black ink printer.

To save on postage of your invitations, the U.S. Postal Service is starting to offer discounts for mail sent nearby. You can also get volume discounts or purchase Express Mail online at a discount at **www. usps.com**.

Save on food

Your party food can be delicious and bountiful without busting your budget. Visit your local Smart and Final store **www.smartandfinal.com**, Costco **www.costco.com**, or Sam's Club **www.samsclub. com** for party-size portions and wine. World Market **www.worldmarket.com** is fun for unusual gourmet items. If you are fortunate and have a Trader Joe's store **www.traderjoes.com** nearby, you will find gourmet food, great wine and alcohol at bargain prices.

Save on party decorations

Visit party supply stores in your area, such as Party City **www.partycity.com** and Party America **www.partyamericastore.com**. Search the Internet, including Evite **www.evite.com** for inexpensive ideas for party themes, food, decorations, and table favor ideas. If a birthday is near a holiday, use that holiday as your theme. For example, Heidi's birthday is just before Valentine's Day, one of her favorite holidays.

Stores such as Michaels **www.michaels.com** and Joann Fabric and Craft Stores **www.joann.com** also have crafts for making invitations, place cards, decorations, and centerpieces. IKEA **www.ikea.com**

has inexpensive, clever table gifts, centerpiece ideas and creative lighting suggestions.

Decorate chairs with wide bows made with strips of fabric that match or coordinate with the tablecloths, table runners and napkins that you make. You don't need a sewing machine, just a good pair of scissors. Find fabric sales at stores such as Joann Fabric and Craft Stores and decorator fabric stores such as Calico Corners **www.calicocorners.com**. Also, the Internet lists dozens of fabric sources.

Here's an idea for the easiest and showiest floral display for your centerpiece or coffee table: Go to your local farmers' market and buy an armload of lilies. Asian lilies last a long time. Buy buds that are still closed up. Clip the bottoms of the stems, keep the water fresh, and they will open up in time for your party, fill the room with fragrance, and last for a week or two.

Save on decorating for your party

If your party inspires you to give your house a facelift, you can do it easily if you have a sewing machine and can sew a straight line. Create pillow covers, drapes, duvet covers, and throw-blankets. You can cover an ugly wall or odd view with a drapery that covers the entire wall.

Paint gives an inexpensive but creative new look. Your local community college will have helpful decorating classes, such as painting decorative faux finishes. Buy attractive but inexpensive area rugs at Lowe's **www.lowes.com** or Home Depot **www.homedepot.com**. Buy dried flower arrangements at craft stores such as Michaels **www.michaels.com**, Joann Fabric and Craft Stores **www.joann.com** and Wal-Mart **www.walmart.com.** Shop annual sales at furniture stores for unusual accessories. Watch television channels about home decorating such as

HGTV (Home and Garden TV) **www.hgtv.com,** and DIY (Do It Yourself Network) **www.diynetwork. com**.

Stick to your party budget

Set your budget for your party and stick to it. You can always substitute less expensive items or eliminate items, to match up with your bottom line.

Sam's parties are larger and more formal. If he uses a caterer, banquet manager, or party planner, he sets the budget with them in advance and makes them stick to it. Keep in mind that banquet coordinators are usually paid on commission. That means that the more money they convince you to spend, the more money they make for themselves. Therefore, they have very little motivation to keep your costs down.

Before you sign any contracts for your party, make sure you are signing a list of every detail about what the banquet site is agreeing to do for you. The contract should clearly state what you are buying and the total amount to which you are agreeing. After you sign, if you object to or want to change anything, they will pull out a copy of the contract. It all has to be in the contract, so get it all writing before you sign anything and keep your copy handy.

Substitute when you can

Be sure to consider all possible food and flower options. You can have high appeal with low cost if you are creative. For example, if certain fruits and flowers you want are out of season, they will cost more. Find out what fruits and flowers are in season and work with them instead. (This is a good idea, even if you aren't planning a party.)

You can also save on desserts. Many banquet hall suggest an elaborate dessert. Sam has observed, however, that about half to three-quarters of the guests don't eat their desert or they only take a bite or two. If it's a birthday or anniversary, have a big cake that is then cut into modest-size pieces. Let the hotel or banquet hall know that you do not want the pieces cut too large. Then welcome guests to come to the cake table and take a piece of cake if they want it. If there is cake left over, the catering staff can circle the room with trays of cake pieces. Many guests will refuse to take the cake because they are too busy talking, too full from dinner, or on a diet. There's no need for you to pay for beautiful, overpriced desserts that will be tossed in the trash barrel.

For weddings, of course, don't offer a dessert in addition to the wedding cake. That would be "sweet-tooth overkill."

Know how many for whom to book the room

When you make reservations for a large party or wedding, you may be concerned about how many guests will actually show up. Event planners know that, unfortunately, roughly 10% to 15% of the people who say they will attend do not actually show up. Here is a tip that can save you lots of money on your event budget. Banquet halls often allow you an additional 10% leeway on the number of guests they serve. Check with your banquet coordinator.

Let's say you are expecting 198 guests. Don't make the reservation for 198 guests. Here's why: if you book the hall for 180 guests, the hall will be prepared to serve 198, an additional 10%. If more than 180 arrive, you pay for each additional meal individually, per person.

This costs less than agreeing to pay for 198 guests and have fewer than 198 of the guests show up, because you would have to pay for 198 dinners, even if fewer guests arrive.

Know how to get a bargain

Not all of Sam's social events have been lavishly catered affairs. He ran an off-campus boarding house one year while he was a student at Stanford University. To raise extra money for the boarding house, he offered a Saturday night "all you can eat" dinner for about 125 people. The boarding house served spaghetti with meat sauce, garlic bread, salad, and a mug full of beer (but the students had to bring their own mug). Sam bought hamburger in bulk for 10¢ a pound and cheddar cheese for 10¢ a pound. The charge for dinner was $1.25, but the cost of the food was less than 50¢ per meal.

For a change of pace, he bought lamb ribblets on sale for 10¢ a pound. To make them edible, he marinated then overnight in teriyaki soy sauce and broiled them. The boarding house got four orders to a pound and sold them for 25¢ per order. They sold an average of $1.00 worth of ribblets to each of the Saturday night guests. Those little ribblets added up to big profits by the end of the evening.

That was in 1954. Even today, however, buying in bulk and being creative with your menu can result in an elaborate affair at a reasonable price.

Ask the pros for advice

When you start planning your party, know the number of people you expect to attend and what kind of food you want to serve. Then ask the store managers for advice about what to serve and how to prepare it.

You never know who will come to your rescue. For example, while at Stanford, Sam belonged to a club on campus. One year, the club was required to host about 900 people for an alumni reception after one of the football games. The club had only $100 in its bank account. The club members visited the campus commissary cooks to ask for help. There they learned about a "Kool Aid" type powder they could buy in bulk for about $20. It made enough punch to serve 900 people. They purchased napkins and paper cups at a discount store and spent about $5 on fresh fruit. In those days $5 could buy quite a few apples, oranges, and peaches. They cut the fruit into small pieces and sprinkled it on the top of the punch.

The event cost less than $100. The Alumni Association said it was one of the most successfully catered receptions that any campus organization had put on for them, even though some of the other receptions had a budget that was ten times larger.

It's not how much you spend for fun;
it's how much fun you have.

Chapter 17

HOW TO BE A THRIFTY SHOPPER

*"A cynic is a man who knows the price of everything
and the value of nothing."*
—Oscar Wilde

Most people have lots of experience in shopping, but not everyone knows the best ways to shop. Here's how to increase the value of your purchases while decreasing the amount that you spend on them.

Search for value

Know value when you find it; just don't pay full price for it. Buy real value, not flashy packaging. Invest your money in long-term quality, not temporary prestige. Don't be fooled into thinking that designer brand items are higher in quality. An item doesn't necessarily increase in value just because it has a label. This holds true for almost everything, including jewelry, furniture, tableware, linens, and cars.

Some things have real value and are worth the price. On that list are healthful food and comfortable shoes, beds, and furniture.

Analyze your purchase

Whenever you find something you want, analyze it closely before you buy. Don't forget to adopt TheSmartestWay™ philosophy and ask yourself: "Do I really need this?" "Is it priced well?" "Is it made well?" "Can I afford it?" "Will I use it often?" "Does it work with other things I own?" "Will I be able to use it several years from now?" "Does it really have value for me?"

If you answer "no" to any of these questions, don't buy it.

Sam's stories about value

Sam learned to look for real value when he was young. Once he visited his cousin, who was working as a butcher in a supermarket. In the display case was ground sirloin for $1.50 per pound and hamburger for $1.00 per pound. Sam asked his cousin, "What is the difference between the ground sirloin and the hamburger?" His cousin replied, honestly, "50¢ a pound."

Sam's father was a manufacturer of vitamins for most of the major drug chains on the West Coast. One of his customers was a high-end, exclusive pharmacy located in medical buildings who sold his multi-vitamin formula in a green capsule for $16 a bottle. Another customer was a large chain of discount drug stores. They sold the same multi-vitamins in a red capsule for $8 a bottle. Each bottle contained the same number of capsules. Sam once asked his father, "What is the difference between what the pharmacy is selling and what the discount drug store is selling?" His father replied simply, "One capsule is green and the other is red." From this, Sam learned that the most expensive is not always better.

Think before you spend

Shop with a list. Shop intentionally, not aimlessly. Before you buy, think *TheSmartestWay*™. "Is this purchase going to help me save money in the long run?" "Is this the best use of my money right now?" "Does this purchase serve my long-range desires?" "Will it help me advance in my career?" "What am I trying to accomplish with this purchase?"

Ask for the bargain price

If you don't ask, you don't get. Sam's wife always asks the "magic" question, "What can you do for us on this?" Then she asks a second time, just as politely, "Isn't there something more you can do?"

It may feel a bit awkward at first, but you'll start to get a thrill from the "magic" results of simply asking. With each new perk or discount that you receive, you will become more confident and remember to ask more often.

According to a recent study, over 90% of people who asked for a discount received at least one. This technique even applies to legal and medical bills. Don't be too proud to let your doctors and lawyers know that you need them to please "shave a little off the top" of their bill. Many hospitals will work with you on payment plans, too.

Most expensive items have a large markup in price. The store can give you anywhere from a 5% to a 15% discount. On luxury items, such as jewelry, the discount may reach upwards to 50%–60%. But they won't give it to you unless you ask!

As for jewelry, it's difficult to know if it will increase in value over time. If you have a desire for fine jewelry, take a look at whether it is really the best use of your money or if you can make a more profitable investment.

Know who to ask and how to ask

You are more likely to get a discount when dealing with the owner or manager of a store rather then with one of the clerks. It always pays to ask, "Can you do better?" Stay upbeat but persistent. Keep your demands high but realistic. If you escalate your demands and become irrational, the seller will politely withdraw from the negotiation.

Try to buy expensive items at discount stores. The savings can be substantial, but you need to make sure that it is a true discount. Compare the discount price with the lowest price you can get from a regular store. Sears **www.sears.com**, JC Penney **www.jcpenney. com**, Mervyn's **www.mervyns.com**, Kohl's **www. kohls.com** and other discount stores are good places to start comparison shopping.

For appliances, ask a contractor what is the most reliable and properly priced brand for your needs. Choose a reliable brand for the price.

In some cases, the store may not be able to offer you a discount on the item itself but will have floor samples or discontinued models. The floor models may have a slight defect that doesn't affect the purpose, appearance, or usefulness of the item. The same is sometimes true with clothing in a department store.

Remember, the sales associate or manager from whom you are asking a bargain has to answer to his boss, too. Find out what's in it for him and be sensitive to his motivations. For example, is he supposed to clear the store of merchandise before inventory? Perhaps he is not allowed to give you a discount on the model you want, but he can discount an older model. You often don't need the very newest model of electronics and other items. Usually the slightly older model is good enough and perhaps even more reliable. It has been out on the market longer and tested by more users.

Use senior discounts

Speaking of buying things at a discount, don't forget that when you reach age fifty-five, you qualify for the senior discount at some movie theatres and restaurants. An increasing number of stores and movie theatres provide discounts for people over age sixty-five, students or veterans. Are you part of a group that receives discounts? If so, don't be embarrassed to ask for what you are entitled. Heidi points out that you could save enough to buy popcorn. Sam says, skip the popcorn and add the money to your investment account!

Shop early—or late

Often you can save on airline tickets and hotel reservations by buying early. You can choose from a better selection if you go to garage sales and flea markets early in the morning. You may find something that you like that seems overpriced.

Here's a great trick: come back at the end of the day and offer a lower price, if it is still there. Quite often the seller will deeply discount anything that is left at the end of the day. When visiting a trade show, the same is often true of merchandise that is left at the end of the show. The vendor may not want to take it home and will either give it away or sell it at a deep discount.

There are other situations where buying as late as possible can save a great deal of money. A good example is a new car or major appliance. You can usually get a good discount if you buy your car at the end of the model year. That's when the new models are about to come out and the dealer is eager to clear out the older models.

Shop at the end of the holiday season for incredible savings. The best time to buy any holiday items is the day after that holiday. The selection is good and the prices are even better—usually half off or more. Stock up for next year's decorations and handy gifts.

The best time to buy office supplies is in August at back to school sales. Almost everything is on sale at office supply stores at that time.

Shop at dollar stores and farmers' markets

As mentioned earlier, try out your local dollar stores like 99 Cent Only stores **www.99only.com**, Dollar Stores **www.dollarstore.com** and Dollar Tree Stores **www.dollartree.com**. These stores contain lots of everyday products and tools on which you can save money. They also have lots of gift and holiday items. As always, be sure to examine your purchases carefully to make sure they are of sufficient quality.

At farmers' markets, sometimes the prices are higher than at a grocery store. But often the produce is fresher and some of it may be organic.

Shop for sales

It also pays to wait for sales. Sam buys his shirts and suits from a very high-end department store that has sales twice a year. By waiting for the sales, he usually saves 25%–30%. When he sees an item that he needs, he asks when it will be on sale and when the next sale is scheduled. Put the sales on your calendar and start compiling a list of the items that you need to shop for at those sales.

Look for stores that are going out of business or liquidating inventory. But before you go crazy with sales, become a shopper *TheSmartestWay*™ and first decide: "Am I really saving money on things I need? Or am I using the sale as an excuse to buy things I don't need?"

Some stores, including bookstores such as Borders Books **www.borderstores.com**, have specific sales areas or tables of bargain-priced items. Look for special areas designated for discounted merchandise. Many furniture stores, such as IKEA **www.ikea.com**, have a special section for sale items.

January is a great month for sales because stores try to get rid of last year's and holiday merchandise.

Comparison shop

Do your research before you lay down your hard-earned money for big-ticket items such as electronics and cars. Ask people whom you respect for their recommendations. If they have already purchased the item, ask them *TheSmartestWay*™ questions: How do they like it? Do they wish that they had bought a different model? Where did they find the best bargain? Also check *Consumer Reports* magazine and online at **www.consumerreports.org** to find information and ratings about all kinds of products.

Comparison shop for bargains on the Internet, too. In your search engine, put in the product you are looking for and the word "discount." Numerous sites will appear. Also, some websites help you find all the discount sites for each kind of product you may be seeking. Remember, good quality can be obtained at a good price.

When you enter a store, take a good look around and see everything. Then compare with other stores before you make a decision. Make sure you are getting the best value and you are getting what you really want for the funds that you have available.

Almost every weekend, Sam likes to comparison shop at local farmers' markets, swap meets, and flea markets. These are places where lots of vendors are selling similar merchandise, but the vendors located closest to the entrance of the market usually charge a higher price than those who are more distant from the entrance. So Sam cruises through the entire market making mental notes about products and prices before he buys anything. He always saves money by comparison shopping first.

Keep price tags and receipts

Keep the receipts for your purchases. Keep the original boxes, bags, and wrapping. And don't cut off price tags, until you are really sure that you want to keep the item. When you buy shoes, test them out at home, but wear them only on carpet or rugs so you don't scuff the soles.

You may find the same item the next day for substantially less or a better item for less. Keep your options open as long as possible. If you are making a sizeable purchase, get the name of the sales associate. That way, you can go back to him or her if you have a problem, question, or need to make a return.

Sometimes, gift givers are courteous enough to give you a "gift receipt" when they give you a gift. You should do the same. This allows the receiver to return the item to the store and buy something else. No one should feel guilty about exchanging gifts. It's better for everyone to be happy about the gift rather than to keep something just in order to not hurt anyone's feelings.

Ask for what you deserve

You must learn to be a proactive, assertive consumer. Don't be afraid to return merchandise that you don't want for fear that a sales associate may dislike you or act rudely to you. Remember, you are the customer and in retail, "The customer is king (or queen)."

Be bold when you ask for a refund for faulty merchandise. It's not your fault if the merchandise is unsatisfactory, so don't apologize for it. Also, you have the right to demand that unapproved charges be removed from your credit card bill. Someone else made the error and they need to correct it.

You won't get what you deserve unless you ask. So ask.

Beware of buying extended warranties

Extended warranties are frequently offered on appliances and technology devices. Stores love to offer them because they represent $9 billion in sales every year. However, on average, for every 100 warranties sold, only 15 people make claims. Take your time before deciding on an extended warranty.

If the item is low cost and you could buy a new one for close to the price of the warranty, don't buy the warranty. Sometimes the warranty may cost more than the repairs would be if you were to need them. For example, major appliances usually are so well made that they seldom need repairs during the life of the extended warranty.

Check to make sure that your item already has a manufacturer's coverage for the first thirty days or the first year. You usually have thirty days to decide to purchase a warranty if you change your mind and decide to buy one. Ask the sales associate about this.

Beware of "early entrants"

An "early entrant" is the first offer of the fresh-from-the-factory model. Often the first introduction of an item is priced higher than it will be if you wait awhile. Waiting a little can save you a lot on computers, iPods, cell phones, flat screen televisions and audio equipment.

> ***It's not what you buy;***
> ***it's how you shop.***

Chapter 18

WHERE TO SHOP TO FIND GOOD DEALS

"Almost any man knows how to earn money,
but not one in a million knows how to spend it. **"**
—Henry David Thoreau

Our country is filled with malls and stores; the options can seem limitless. Where you shop determines if you will find what you need—and save money at the same time.

Shop at "big box" stores

There are usually some nice surprises at "big box" discount stores such as Sam's Club **www.samsclub. com**; BJs **www.bjs.com,** and Costco **www.costco. com**. Don't be too proud to visit your local Wal-Mart **www.walmart.com** (800-WALMART), Target **www.target.com,** and Smart and Final **www. smartandfinal.com**. They also carry top quality home products, grooming basics, gift items, and casual clothes. Ask the manager for any discounts that aren't advertised. Try the "generic" store brands. Much of the merchandise in these kinds of stores is sold in larger quantities and at significant savings.

Heidi stocks up on large quantities of everyday kitchen, bathroom, and other household items, such as paper towels, facial tissue, bathroom tissue, trash bags, detergent for clothes and dishes, sandwich bags, etc. She has a pantry area in which to store them.

We want to point out that just because something is sold in quantity at a volume discount at a big box store, that doesn't mean that it's a true "bargain" for you. Don't let the "bargain effect" cloud your judgment. The "bargain effect" may alter your buying decisions by convincing you to stock up on items that you don't really need or buy quantities that you can't really use just because they are on sale. This is a waste of your money. On the other hand, maybe you can split the multiple quantities with a friend or neighbor.

Nevertheless, big box discount stores have a lot to offer.

Shop at discount districts

Often a slightly longer drive to a wholesale clothing or jewelry district is worth the extra time and money spent on gas. The "mark up"—the increase in price from wholesale to retail—is significant. The price of jewelry is usually much lower in the jewelry district. With jewelry, the mark up is sometimes 400%.

Use clubs, catalogs, discount cards

Many grocery stores, drug stores, bookstores, and other retailers offer customers a "frequent customer" discount card. Some have an annual charge for the membership, but most are free. For stores that charge, decide if the annual charge will be worth it based on how often you shop at the store and how much you will save with the discounts. If you forget or misplace your discount card, many stores will have the information in their database or swipe a generic card for you, so that you get the discount.

Shop at garage sales, thrifts shops, etc.

Garage sales and swap meets are fun places to pick up odds and ends that you need. "One person's trash is another person's treasure." Consignment shops that sell furniture or clothes provide great shopping.

Keep in mind that you too can sell your unwanted items this way, or through an advertisement in the classifieds section of your newspaper and the Penny Saver catalogs. "Turn your trash into cash" and resell the extra stuff in your life that is weighing you down and holding you back. "Monetize" those items so you can buy things you really need or trade them for things you can really use. The Internet offers trading and swapping opportunities, such as on Craig's List **www. craigslist.org**. Even items that would be difficult to sell can be converted to cash savings by donating them to a qualified charity and taking a tax deduction for their value. Also look at **www.freecycle.com**.

Thrift stores and pawn shops can be worthwhile, depending on the location. Generally, the nicer neighborhoods have better merchandise. For example, thrift stores and pawn shops in or near very upscale areas, such as Beverly Hills offer amazing deals.

Don't forget your local library. You can check out movies, DVDs, CDs, audio tapes and books for free. Some libraries may sell these items at low prices. Many are like new, and some are often in their original wrapping.

Shop at auctions

Auctions are a great way to find bargains or to get rid of things you don't want anymore. Here are Sam's favorite techniques for shopping at auctions:

1. Be sure to see the item before you bid on it. Often the item will look good at first glance, but have significant defects upon closer inspection. Analyze the item up close to see if it has real value or use for you.

2. Avoid buying on impulse. Know before you attend the auction on which items you are going to bid. You can usually get a catalog or review the items to be offered on the Internet. Once you start bidding, don't let your pride get in the way of your common sense. It's easy to become competitive while bidding. The goal is to get a good deal, not to beat the other bidders. The longer you bid, the harder it is to stop. Decide ahead of time the top price you are willing to pay. Bring a friend or relative and ask them to give you a light tap when your top price is reached.

3. Develop a "poker face." A poker face is the expression used when someone is playing poker and they want to hide their emotions about how good or bad their cards are. In other words, don't indicate to the other bidders if you are glad or disappointed about how the bidding is going. Also, don't indicate what your top price is. The simplest way is to start your bid low and raise the price the minimum amount allowed.

4. Know if there is a premium. Many auctions require what is called "a buyer's premium," which ranges from 10% to 20%. For example, if the buyer's premium was 20%, for each $1.00 you bid, you would pay $1.20.

5. Remember sales tax. Unless you have a resale license and are planning to resell the item, you must also pay sales tax on the buyer's premium. Therefore, if you bid $100 and the buyer's premium is 20%, with sales tax of 6% the item will cost you $127.20.

6. Remember to include income taxes on what you must earn to pay for everything you purchase. As we explain elsewhere, you have to earn 160% of the price of any item you buy in order to have the necessary funds to purchase the item. That's why income taxes consume so much of your money.

7. Remember shipping and repair costs. If the item is large and you need to transport it, be sure that you have the money to do so or know what it will cost to move it from the auction site to your home. If repairs are needed, have a good estimate of how much they will cost.

8. Disregard the auctioneer. Pay no attention to his or her claims about how wonderful and valuable the item is. The only thing that matters is what value it has for you and if you really need it.

9. Get there early. The auction may run all day if there are lots of items. Find out from the auction staff approximately when the item is scheduled to come up for sale. Arrive at the auction at least one half hour prior to your item's scheduled bid time. That will give you time to examine the item closely one more time to make sure that it is still in good condition and free of defects.

10. Find out about storage. If you are not going to take the item with you the day of the auction, ask how many days you have before you have to pick it up and where it will be located. Often it will be sent to a different location to be stored.

11. Try phone bidding. At the preview you may be able to arrange to bid by phone by filling out a form. This saves you the time and expense of another trip to the auction house.

Shop to upgrade your home

If you're in the market for furniture, IKEA **www.ikea.com** (800-434-IKEA) has great deals on furniture, kitchen, and bathroom cabinetry, plus home accessories. If you want to remodel your home, try to find a contractor or handyman who is willing to help you on his off-hours, evenings, and weekends, at a reduced hourly rate or project rate.

For your home office, Best Buy **www.bestbuy.com** offers bargains on technology. So does Costco, Staples **www.staples.com**, Office Max **www.officemax.com** and Office Depot **www.officedepot.com**. The discounted floor models may be just what you need at the price you want. Office supply stores also have comfortable, ergonomic desk and office chairs.

It's not where you shop;
it's what you get.

Chapter 19

HOW TO SAVE MONEY ON CLOTHES

"What a lot of things there are a man can do without."
—Socrates

L et's face it. Most of us don't need more clothes. Most of us have enough clothes to last a long time. Still, shopping for clothes has become a popular hobby. Men, women and children flock to the malls in droves in perpetual pursuit of the "perfect" wardrobe. Advertisements tout "must-have" accessories and "to-die-for" shoes.

Figure out why clothes are so important

Have you ever asked yourself: "Why are clothes so important to me?" Some of us have motivations about our clothes that come from our childhood. Take Heidi, for example. Her mother grew up during the Depression as the youngest of nine in a thrifty, Montana farming family of Scotch descent. They knew how to make a lot from a little.

Heidi's mother encouraged her interest in fashion when she was a little girl. She would sew up unique, "couture" creations from leftover fabric whenever Heidi's Barbie dolls needed a new look. She bought Heidi dresses, petticoats, and pumps from the Salvation Army. They dyed and decorated them with ribbons and buttons for her to wear when she played "dress up."

Heidi's aunt generously mailed huge boxes full of clothes that she had lovingly sewn for her two daughters. But Heidi hated wearing "hand-me-downs" and she yearned to be "in style" and wear new clothes like the other girls at school. Her determination as a little girl grew until, as a young woman, she eventually fulfilled her dream and became an editor of two fashion publications.

Understand that you aren't what you wear

Women are especially alert to the fact that what we wear says a lot about us. But just like our car—we aren't what we drive—and we aren't what we wear either. Sometimes, it's easy to get confused about this. Here's a story related to this concept that is unfortunately all too common.

Recently a major Hollywood personality needed advice on her financial affairs. She had received a substantial income for many years, but was troubled that she had not been able to acquire any profitable investments. She confessed to her advisor that in the previous year she had spent approximately 40% of her annual after-tax income of several million dollars on clothes. She told herself that she needed the clothes for "keeping up her image."

This story reminds Sam of the quote from another actress who was once asked, "Are you living within your income?" She replied, "No, it's all I can do to live within my credit."

Know where to indulge in the thrill of the hunt

Heidi has discount-shopping in her DNA. Her mother has always prided herself in her very attractive, thrift-store/yard-sale discoveries.

If you know where to shop, you can stretch your wardrobe budget. Everyone likes high quality and designer labels. (Actually those aren't always the same thing.). You'll be delighted with the high quality and low prices if you shop during sales and at discount stores and designer outlets. These days, you can get designer quality without the designer price. What's not to like about that?

Nordstrom, known for high quality and fashion, has an outlet store called Nordstrom Rack. Find the location nearest you online at **www.nordstrom.com** and click on the link to The Rack or call (888-282-6060). The Rack sells lots of Nordstrom merchandise and has super discounts on quality underwear, shoes, clothes, and accessories for men and women. The fashions may be only a few weeks or months behind the latest fashion trends of the season. The Rack is Heidi's favorite place to shop for clothes. Also, she likes to visit outlet malls that have many designer stores. Designer outlet malls are located throughout the country. Often the quality is the same as the branded merchandise found at non-outlet stores.

You'll find quality clothes at discount stores such as TJ Maxx **www.tjmaxx.com** (800-962-MAXX), Loehmann's **www.loehmanns.com,** Marshall's **www.marshallsonline.com** (800-MARSHALLS), Target **www.target.com** (800-440-0680), Stein Mart **www.steinmart.com**; Burlington Coat Factory **www.burlingtoncoatfactory.com,** Kohl's **www.kohls.com** (866-887-8884), Mervyns **www.mervyns.com** (800-MERVYNS), JC Penney **www.jcpenney.com**

(800-322-1189), Sears **www.sears.com**, and Ross Dress for Less **www.rossdressforless.com**.

As we mentioned before, you can find casual clothes at big savings at "big box" stores such as Sam's Club **www.samsclub.com**; Wal-Mart **www.walmart. com**, (800-WALMART); BJ's **www.bjs.com**; and Costco **www.costco.com**.

For shoes, you can quickly try on a dozen of pair of shoes and find the perfect pair if you shop at a shoe warehouse. The selection is broad and the prices low. Many of these stores, such as DSW Shoes **www. dswshoes.com**, carry designer shoes and handbags at good discounts. The Rack also carries a large selection of designer shoes in large and wide sizes.

None of these stores are glamorous, but the merchandise can be incredible. Have no doubt, you can stay "in style" while discount shopping.

At this writing, these are some of the types of stores that we recommend that you investigate. Retail is an industry of change and some of these stores may be replaced by others in the future.

Strategize your clothes shopping

Heidi has a "plan of attack" for finding clothes at discount clothing stores. First, she wears a close-fitting T-shirt or camisole. When she enters the store, she grabs a shopping cart, courses through the store and fills the cart with sweaters, shirts and tops she might like. She finds a large mirror in the store and tries on the tops over her T-shirt. Then she searches for pants and skirts that match the tops she likes. Those are taken to the dressing room to see if they fit. If she doesn't find tops and bottoms to match each other or match something she already has, she doesn't buy them.

If you have to try the clothes on in a "communal" dressing room, just swallow your pride and have some fun with it. Often, fellow shoppers offer their honest opinion of how you look.

Use the 10 Question Test

Whenever Heidi finds an item she might like, she puts it through the 10 Question Test. If she gets lots of "yeses" to the questions below, she puts it in her cart to try it on.

1) Do I really need this item?
2) Is it priced well for the value?
3) Can I afford the expense right now?
4) Would I wear it lots of places?
5) Would I wear it often?
6) Does it fit the image I'm trying to project?
7) Does it coordinate with my other clothes?
8) Is it made well enough to last several years?
9) Would I wear it several years from now?
10) Would I regret not buying it?

If Heidi find items she likes that fit, she asks a store clerk to put them "on hold." Most stores are willing to keep items in the back room with your name on it until closing time that day. After Heidi places the items on hold, she leaves the store and runs another errand. If she's still thinking about the items an hour or two later, she might return to the store to buy them.

Develop your own style

A consistent style in your wardrobe enhances your personal image. It also requires fewer clothes. Experiment with and note which shapes and styles look best on you. Then make a list of the clothes you really need for work and home and shop for those items when the season is right and the sales are on. Build a wardrobe that is useful, unique, and makes you look and feel great. As you develop your own personal wardrobe style, you'll learn to "brand" your individual look and enjoy dressing and shopping.

As a little girl, Heidi shopped for her clothes from the JC Penney catalog. As a young woman, she landed a job as a personal shopper for Nordstrom. There, she learned about quality and lasting style. Over time, she developed her own style that might be called California classic with a creative flair. The flair comes from her work in fashion writing.

Customize your look

Heidi accents her classic styled suits with trendier accessories such as scarves, unusual lapel pins and necklaces and bracelets. She buys her pins from vintage clothing shops and chunky stone and metal jewelry on sale at Chico's **www.chicos.com**. If she buys a garment with boring buttons, she replaces them with fashionable buttons from Joann Fabric and Craft Stores **www.joann.com**. She hires a seamstress to make colorful blouses and tops from fabric that she finds at Joann stores and at discount decorator fabric stores. A good seamstress can make an exact pattern from any garment.

Men can update and individualize their wardrobe with ties and shirts in trendy colors. If you find a piece of fabric that would make a great tie or shirt, take it to your tailor. Now you have a one-of-a-kind, signature piece that cost a fraction of what you would have paid at the store.

Sam is a businessman in the conservative worlds of finance and law, so he always wears a suit and tie to the office. He was educated in the Northern California Bay

Area, which is much more conservative than Southern California. In Southern California, business attire is more relaxed, so Sam wears pale-colored shirts and pocket squares that match his tie.

Stick to the basics

We recommend that you build a long-lasting wardrobe of quality pieces in basic silhouettes and styles. This is the core of your wardrobe—your suits, blazers, pants (and skirts if you're a woman). Choose from a neutral palette of black, gray, dark or light brown, navy, khaki, camel, tan, beige and cream. Then select a couple of basic accent colors, such as red and royal blue or wine and teal.

To update your look every year, add a few pieces in "trendy" colors to accent your basics. These pieces can be ties and casual shirts for men, tops and accessories for women. Some trendy colors are orange, lemon, lime, pale pink, rose, magenta, lavender, purple, or turquoise.

If you buy good quality, the core of your wardrobe won't need to be replaced as often. Buy fewer clothes but better clothes. Heidi has clothes she has worn for more than twenty years, and she still gets compliments on them. Sam buys well-made suits (on sale) so he can wear them for many years.

Master the fashion trends; don't be a slave to them. Analyze each item to decide if it coordinates with your current wardrobe, enhances your individual style and fits your wardrobe budget.

Stay the same weight

Speaking of being consistent, one of the best things you can do for your wardrobe budget is to keep your weight the same. You can build one wonderful wardrobe, not two so-so wardrobes—your "fat" wardrobe and your "skinny" wardrobe.

Care for your wardrobe

Try to buy machine-washable clothes whenever possible to save on dry cleaning bills. If the label recommends dry cleaning, be sure to do so. Otherwise, you may ruin the garment. But if you're brave, you can try laundering certain "dry clean only" items. Hand wash them in the sink with gentle soap, lay them out smooth on a towel, or hang them up to dry on a hanger. Stains come out easier with Simple Green household cleaner (full strength) and Soil Love (available at 99 Cents Only Stores).

Heidi visits a shoe repair shop to have her favorite shoes resoled. She's had them for years because they are comfortable, classic, and still in style. The shoe repair shop can dye her shoes and handbags to match each other or coordinate with a specific outfit. Heidi alters her clothes to give them new life and keep up with fashion. The seamstress at her drycleaner shortens skirts and hems and alters slacks to fit better.

Find a good tailor

The alterations seamstress at your dry cleaners can fix the clothes you already have. But a professional tailor or dressmaker can create custom clothes for you. Heidi designs her professional pant suits with her husband's tailor, who creates George Foreman's suits. She appreciates the quality of custom-made men's suits—the linings, the tailoring, the covered buttons. She likes to choose from thousands of colors and patterns of fine fabrics and dozens of design styles. They are one-of-a-kind and fit to perfection. The best part is her suits cost far less than suits at Nordstrom or other fine stores!

Get beauty products at a discount

For great deals on cosmetics and skincare (for teenage girls, too) consider Avon, **www.avon.com** (212-282-7000). Almost all of Heidi's skin care and cosmetics are purchased on sale from Avon. Their Anew skincare line includes low-priced but high-tech wrinkle reducers, lip plumpers, facial peels, and micro-dermabrasion products. She simply emails her representative who lets her know when her favorite products go on sale.

A woman's hair is her crowning glory. Find the best hairstylist in town, not the most expensive hairstylist. Experiment with how long you can wait between visits to the hairdresser. Heidi keeps her hair long and naturally wavy. Longer hair requires trimming and highlighting less frequently, which saves time and money. Some women color their own hair or have a friend help them.

Heidi recommends trying salon-grade shampoo and conditioner. She finds that higher-quality products help maintain manageability, color, and highlighting. Quality brands can be found at a discount at beauty supply stores.

Scrimp when you can. Try Heidi's low-cost "hot oil treatment" to condition your hair. She simply fills a plastic squeeze bottle with canola cooking oil and a few drops of mint oil extract, both from the grocery store. While in the shower, she massages lots of oil into her hair and covers her hair with a plastic shower cap. After a few minutes, she shampoos out the oil. This simple, inexpensive treatment leaves her hair noticeably fuller, glossier and more manageable. Her at-home "spa treatments" for her skin include exfoliating scrubs, self-tanning creams, and softening lotions containing the ingredient Q10—all from the local drug store.

Try to "get what you pay for"

As we said before, an expensive price tag does not guarantee high quality. You have to be the judge of value versus price. The good news is that with careful shopping, you can get great quality at discount prices.

Nevertheless, sometimes the saying is true, "You get what you pay for." A study was done on high-quality men's dress shirts compared to lower quality. The expensive shirt lasted three times longer than the inexpensive shirt. This illustrates the concept of "cost per wear." Which shirt cost you less, the cheap one that you wore only few times and you had to throw away, or a higher-priced shirt that holds up well so that you can wear many times?

The same is true for shoes. Better quality shoes that are comfortable can actually save you money by lasting longer, creating more comfort, and preventing podiatrist bills for bunions, corns, and injuries due to tripping and slipping. This is true for men as well. Sam has some favorite shoes he has worn for over thirty years that have been re-soled four or five times.

Don't get designer-label crazy

It's not "who" you wear; it's how you look that makes an impression. A designer label is just a piece of cloth—a small piece of cloth that you pay a lot of money for. For example, you can buy a black cashmere sweater for $100 through the Lands End catalog **www. landsend.com** or you can pay ten times more for a similar black cashmere sweater with a designer label. It's your choice.

Sam had a client who purchased most of her clothes at one of the designer "needless mark-up" stores. Across the street was a regularly priced department store. Sam encouraged her to shop at the other store. She found several outfits for less than what she was paying for only one outfit at the higher priced store. She also purchased a wool coat at 10% of the price that she had paid for another coat at the more expensive store. Despite the fact that the less-expensive coat didn't have a designer label, she found this coat was the one she chose to wear most often.

Don't get wedding dress crazy

Wedding dresses can seem so important for the big day. But brides need to keep their financial sanity. Here are some suggestions about how to find your dream dress:

Be sentimental. A mother-of-the-bride or mother-in-law-to-be might want the bride to wear her antique wedding gown. It has a built-in heritage that honors the original wearer and her marriage. The gown could be redesigned, refitted, or updated with the help of a good tailor for far less than the cost of new gown. Plus, it will be one-of-a-kind and have loads of sentimental value.

Be persistent. In her search for the perfect wedding dress to wear when she married Bill, Heidi tried on expensive gowns in many high-end bridal shops, including boutiques in Beverly Hills. She finally found her wedding ensemble at a local boutique. Her floor length, ice-blue satin skirt and corset top with matching seed pearl trim by Alfred Angelo **www.alfredangelo. com** cost only $400, full price, including her stole, satin pumps, and satin clutch, all in dyed-to-match satin.

Be practical. The bride may know someone who wears the same dress size and can lend her wedding dress to her. It could be altered for the occasion with different ribbons or buttons, a lace or netting overskirt, or a different bustle. It's also easy to rent wedding dresses at substantial savings.

Sam, the pragmatist, recommends that brides spend less on their wedding gown and more on the down payment of their new home. Heidi, the romantic, suggests a longer honeymoon!

It's not what you wear;
it's what you pay for what you wear.

Chapter 20

PROTECT YOURSELF FROM SCAMS AND FRAUD

"The best way to save money is to not lose it."
—Les Williams

Scams and frauds are everywhere these days. They will increase as the economy struggles to stabilize. Some of the saddest stories we've ever heard are of people who lost all of their savings in a scam or fraud. Many scams and frauds target the elderly, but all age groups are vulnerable. Smart and educated people fall victim to simple scams and frauds. Even we have almost been fooled a few times. Thank goodness we have been warned to be cautious!

You have "won the chance"—to lose

A common scam is someone emailing you or phoning you to say you have won a lottery or a major prize and that all is required is a small sum for "processing" or paying "local taxes" or some other modest expense. Eventually, there are continuous requests for more money. But each time the victim thinks, "I'll just be patient. I have already put in some money, so a little more won't hurt."

In one case that Sam knows, a retired couple participated in such a scam by initially investing only $13. Slowly, but surely, they were conned into sinking their entire life savings of $360,000 into the scam. All they received in the end was a worthless piece of paper.

It's human nature to become even more committed to staying in a bad investment, even if you become suspicious that it may be a scam. Everyone hates to admit that they made a mistake. It's easy to start thinking, "I'll pull out soon. But I'll stay in until I at least get my money back." This weakness in our nature is a trap for gamblers, too.

The solution is to avoid all scams in the first place.

"Help us rob your bank account" scam

Another scam is the "Nigerian Oil Minister Scam." You are contacted by someone who claims to be a relative of someone who is has hidden away millions of dollars from their own country and they will share their wealth with you for your assistance in retrieving the funds. They may ask for access to your bank account or credit cards. This is how they steal your money.

"Fake check" scam

Another scam that also may have originated in Nigeria is called, according to the U.S. Postal Inspection Service, "the fake check" scam. In 2007 alone, the federal government has seized more than $2 billion worth of fake checks. The real-looking checks are mailed to random consumers with a letter asking them to deposit the checks into their account and wire a lesser amount to the sender. When the victim does as directed, the scam artist's checks bounce and the bank demands all of the funds back—including the money that was sent to the scammer!

Part two of the scam is to send you an email explaining that you have been victim of a fraud, but they will help recover your lost money. Then they try to convince you to give them your bank account or credit card numbers. Don't fall for this, either.

Learn more at **www.fakechecks.com**, the Postal Inspection Service's website to educate the public about check scams.

"You have an IRS refund" scam

The Internal Revenue Service is warning taxpayers about fake emails claming that you will receive a refund if you respond with your personal information. Don't ever give your personal information to any unsolicited email request or phone call.

"Start a home-based business" schemes

Unfortunately, the Internet is filled with work-from-home schemes. Many of these offers require a small "deposit" before you can get started in the "business." Too many times, after the deposit is paid the buyer is given nothing and can't do much about it.

Ponzi schemes

In a Ponzi scheme, the person who creates the scheme actually pays out large returns to the first few people who join. As the word spreads of their "success," more people join and more money comes in. This new money is used to pay the early investors. As the scheme grows, the number of investors increases until the scheme collapses because there are too many investors to be paid off from the pool of money.

Those that come in at the end lose their entire investment, those who come in the middle may have gotten some of their money back and those who were early investors probably benefited well, but they are a small number compared to the total participants. A chain letter often works in the same way. Those who start the chain are doing well, while those who come in later lose because the scheme has burned out.

Recognize scams and schemes

Be wary of offers that:

- originate from someone you do not know.
- sound too good to be true.
- come to your attention via email or the phone, or classified ads
- are taped onto telephone poles.
- require a deposit or payment from you to get started.
- use words like, "This is not a chain letter/scam/ scheme…"

You must constantly be alert so that you don't become a victim. Sam has been consulted in cases where the victim was introduced to the scam by a relative, friend, or neighbor who were themselves taken in. He has had close associates and friends swear that the proposition they are presenting to him is totally legitimate. How did they know? One of their friends reportedly had successfully participated. But each case he investigated, without exception, was a scam. He also was never able to track down any person who actually participated successfully in any scam, other than early in a Ponzi scheme. Note that participation in such a scheme is a crime in many jurisdictions and could subject you to prosecution.

Don't be a potential victim

Recently, Heidi almost fell for a scam. She received a phone call offering to reduce her long-distance charges. The cordial caller explained that a rebate was due on her monthly phone bill. They only needed to confirm her name and address in order to process the rebate. She was transferred to a "supervisor" for verification of approval. Then the supervisor asked her for her date of birth. When Heidi hesitated, she was told "or you can give us your mother's maiden name or the last four digits of your Social Security number." Fortunately, Heidi recognized this call was a scam. She said, "No way! Don't ever call me again!" and hung up.

Don't toss it all away with "the roll of the dice"

Avoid all scams, including gambling—the biggest scam of all. "Playing the odds," whether gambling or the lottery, is not the way to create financial stability. The best way to win with money is to invest it wisely. Playing games with your money is not investing it wisely.

You may believe in your heart that you can win your fortune through gambling and playing the lottery. But these "games of chance" are guaranteed to be weighed against you. Have you ever wondered why casinos are so large and lavish? It's because gamblers gave them so much money!

Don't throw away everything for which you've worked so hard. Statistically, you are more likely to be struck by lightning than to win the lottery. To make things worse, a large percentage of lottery winners go bankrupt. This is because they are inexperienced in handling large amounts of money, and they are vulnerable to scams.

Don't get tricked by "free" stuff

Sometimes scammers just want one thing, your email address or your credit card number. They have creative ways to get them. One way is to offer you "free" merchandise.

Think twice before you accept "free" merchandise offered on television, radio, or the Internet. The item may be "free," but you usually have to pay a shipping and handling fee. How do you pay for it? You guessed it—with your credit card.

You will often be asked to give your email address so you can receive coupons and "valuable updates" (that means, advertisements). If you give your email address to the world, the world will be sitting there, waiting for you, every time you check your email.

Also, when you order a product that offers you the first installment or shipment "free," don't forget to call and refuse additional, periodic shipments. They have your credit card number now, so they can continue to ship you and bill you for monthly supplies or installments you don't want and never agreed to pay for. You have to contact the sender to convince them to stop the periodic shipments and refund your credit card charges.

Protect yourself from identity theft

Ten million people are victims of identity theft every year. You could spend hundreds of hours and thousands of dollars to recover your financial identity. Criminals can run up your credit cards, empty your bank accounts, and use your name to take out loans and write bad checks, as well as receive utility services, medical services, and driver's licenses. Losses total between $10 and $20 billion annually.

Protect yourself on the Internet

Fraud via the Internet includes "phishing." This is when fake emails pose as a company you have an account with—for example eBay, PayPal, or your bank—and threaten to close your account unless you immediately email them your user name and password on your account. The website or email may appear to be legitimate and secure. They may claim that they need to "verify a statement" or that you have won a prize or a gift certificate. Legitimate institutions will never ask for this private information, so don't supply it. Do not click on any links, open the document, or even reply to the email. Delete it immediately.

When purchasing online, always log on directly to the website. Shop only on secure websites. Use website addresses that begin with "https." This indicates that your credit card information will be encrypted when it's transmitted over the Internet. Look for the little padlock security icon in the lower right corner. This may indicate that the website is possibly more secure. When you finish making an online purchase, log off that website immediately. If you assign only one credit card for your online shopping, it will be easier to detect if someone else is making charges on that account.

Avoid making online purchases or revealing personal information on your desktop computer or laptop when it is on a wireless connection. This is because nearby computer hackers can tap into your wireless Internet service and steal your information.

Keep all of your passwords top-secret and change them regularly. Use a combination of letters, characters and numbers in the format required by the website. Install anti-virus software and keep it updated daily.

Guard your personal information

Keep your contact information "under the radar" as much as possible. For example, when a store clerk asks for your email address so they can email discount coupons to you, refuse the offer. Don't sign up for raffles to win cars, timeshares, or other prizes at shopping malls. Your contact information could be sold to spammers and telemarketers.

Your contact and credit card information may possibly be downloaded off of hotel digital "swipe" keycards, so destroy those, too.

Don't release information

Be very protective of your personal information:

- Don't give your debit card number, credit card number, bank account number, Social Security number, or ATM pass code to anyone who requests it via an email.
- Don't post your private information on online forums.
- Don't use your Social Security number, address, birth date or ZIP code as a username or password for any pass codes.
- Don't download Internet programs or online links from unknown sources. They may contain hidden fraud programs or viruses embedded in the program.

Also be careful of phone calls from a person or a business you don't know. No one should ask you to make a purchase over the phone or ask about your personal information. If they claim to be calling from the security and fraud department of a credit card company, hang up and call the number on the back of your credit card to verify.

Hang onto your credit cards

Thieves need the personal information in your wallet. Always know where your wallet and handbag are and exactly what's in your wallet. Make photocopies of the credit cards and identification that you carry with you. That way, if your wallet or purse is lost or stolen, you can easily cancel credit cards and bank accounts and replace each item. Carry only a couple of credit cards and a blank check with you. Leave the rest of your credit cards and your checkbook locked up at home. Carry only necessary personal information with you, such as your driver's license. Never carry your Social Security card.

When you make a purchase with your credit card, make sure that you get back your own card. Sometimes the wrong credit card may be returned to you mistakenly. Sometimes it is an intentional scam.

When you acquire a new credit card, do not sign the back. Simply write in the signature space on the back of the card: "check ID." This will require the checkout clerk to ask for your photo ID to match the names on both cards. If someone has stolen your card and their photo identification doesn't match your appearance, they might get caught.

Know that "Big Brother" is watching

Banks have invested large sums of money into sophisticated systems to protect consumers from fraud and theft by monitoring each transaction closely. If any transaction seems "not right," the transaction can be filed, without notice to the consumer, as a Suspicious Activity Report with the Treasury Department's Financial Crimes Enforcement Network.

Citizens are under very close scrutiny, which is designed to protect them and catch wrong-doers. Unfortunately, this scrutiny also infringes on their privacy.

Remove your name from marketing lists

Remove your name from marketing lists. The Direct Marketing Association (DMA) notifies its members that they must remove your name from the lists they sell for five years. Go to **www.dmaconsumers.org**. To reduce the amount of unsolicited mail and catalogs and phone calls from marketers, you can "opt out" by accessing **www.worldprivacyforum.org/toptenoptout.html**.

Guard your mail

Place your outgoing mail in a locked post office box or take it directly to the post office. Make sure that it is not obvious if a check is enclosed. Retrieve your incoming mail as soon as possible. If you move, notify your credit card issuers in advance of your change of address. Know when your billing statements are due. Thieves can request a change of address for your card and run up charges before you realize it.

Use tamper-resistant checks

Purchase tamper-resistant checks from a reputable printer. Don't put your driver's license number or Social Security number on your checks or allow a retailer to write them on the check. Carry checks only when you need them. Store new and cancelled checks safely. When writing checks, use a permanent gel ink that cannot be washed off. One such pen is Uniball Vision Elite. Make sure all gaps are filled in so the amount cannot be altered. Never sign a blank check or credit card receipt.

Use caution at ATMs

If you must use an ATM, have your card handy before you reach the ATM. Make sure that no one is watching you, or photographing you, as you enter your ID number. Put the money away as soon as you get it. Don't count it until you are in a safe place. If you feel wary of the people around the ATM, come back later. Don't use ATMs at night unless someone is with you. If you use a drive-up window ATM, keep the doors locked and the engine running. Always take your receipts with you. Never talk to anyone, help them, or let them help you while at an ATM. If you need cash frequently, ask your local grocery store to give you extra cash back from your credit card or debit card purchases. Avoid unnecessary trips to the bank and possible ATM charges.

Use a shredder

After you finish examining your monthly billing statement, destroy them in a shredder. Many sizes and types of shredders are available at office supply stores. They are not very expensive and are worth the peace of mind. The best shredders cut paper in a cross pattern, rather than in narrow strips. They are called "cross shredders."

Shred, don't toss, every document that contains your name, address and any of your personal information on it. This includes credit card applications, charge slips, deposit slips, financial statements, old credit cards, checks, and receipts.

Follow these easy steps and you won't be an "easy target" for identity thieves who search through trash.

File complaint reports

Report suspicious activity to the Federal Trade Commission (FTC). Forward the original scam email to **www.ftc.gov/spam**. If you believe that you have been the victim of a scam, file your complaint at **www.ftc.gov**.

Check your credit report

You are entitled to a free copy of your credit reports every six months from each of the three major credit bureaus. Contact **www.annualcreditreport.com**. If you use other websites, you may be charged. When you get your report, check it carefully. A recent study found 25% of reports contained serious errors. Contact the credit bureau and clear up the error. Consider signing up at **www.lifelock.com**.

If you are concerned that your identity may have been stolen, you can put a security freeze on your credit reports. This prevents anyone from viewing your credit report. For the latest rules see **www. financialprivacynow.org**.

Get more information

If you think that you've found a scam, check it out on www.snopes.com. The website reports on the latest scams that are being circulated. On the Internet, go to:

- **www.ftc.gov/consumers/consumer/alerts/ phishing.html** for more information on phishing scams,
- **www.ftc.gov/bcp/conline/pubs/credit/ idtheft.htm** for more information on identity theft,
- **www.usps.com/postalinspectors** for the U.S. Postal Inspections Service, and
- **www.usdoj.gov/criminal/fraud/idtheft. html** for the U.S. Justice fraud department.

It's not what you know;
it's what you don't know.

Chapter 21

WHERE DOES IT ALL GO? INFLATION AND TAXES

"There was a time when a fool and his money were soon parted. But now it happens to everybody."
—Adlai Stevenson

I t has been said, "To acquire wealth is not easy, but to keep it is even more difficult." You need to know how to defend your hard-earned funds from factors that erode your wealth. Two of the most powerful factors are inflation and taxes.

Inflation

Understand inflation and plan for it

Inflation is the slowly creeping higher cost of living. It is the increase in the costs of goods and services over time. Quietly, stealthily, inflation takes our money by reducing our purchasing power, so that our dollars don't stretch as far as they did. If your income stays the same, eventually it won't buy as much, partly because of inflation. Similar to taxes, inflation is caused by circumstances beyond our control, including consumer spending rates, government deficits, energy demands, worker productivity fluctuations, and wage levels.

Here's an example of how inflation erodes your wealth. Say the inflation rate isn't too high, just 3%. If you had $10,000 this year, next year, it would be worth $300 less, or only $9,700. In thirty years, the 3% inflation would have eaten 59% of your $10,000, or $4,100. Look at it this way: if the inflation rate was 3% every year, what costs $100 today will cost $103 next year and 3% more each year.

Remember inflation erodes your savings plan. If you save only at the rate of inflation—say 3% per year—you still are just "standing still." You are not really moving ahead or saving.

Taxes

The government taxes the nation's income earners to provide security and social services to its citizens. Frequent changes to the tax laws alter our ability to control our wealth. This variable must always be considered in your savings and investing plan.

Taxes can sneak up on you

Face the sad reality of how taxes affect your money. You may think only of federal income taxes when you think of taxes. Don't forget that we all pay many more taxes, including state income taxes, city income taxes, sales taxes, excise taxes, Social Security taxes (deducted from paychecks) and real estate taxes (on property). When you add all these taxes together, you may be paying close to 50% of your earnings to taxes. That's a huge bite out of your spending capacity!

Don't overlook the fact that the government taxes a bonus as if it were income. That means you first have to set aside the taxes you will have to pay before you decide how to use what is left of the bonus.

Also, as soon as you get a profit from an investment or commission, immediately set aside the amount that will be required to pay taxes.

Taxes drain your income

Someone once asked, only half joking, "Why does a slight tax increase cost you two hundred dollars, but a substantial tax cut only saves you thirty cents?" Taxes are a difficult situation that every citizen has to deal with, like it or not.

We want to explain why taxes take so much of your income. Ready? Here it is: When you buy something for $1.00, it really costs you $1.60. Or you could say that you have to earn $1.60 in order to be able to afford to spend $1.00.

Why is that? It's because of taxes. The $1.00 price you pay when you buy a cheap cup of coffee doesn't take into account the 60 cents in tax that you will eventually have to pay on that $1.00 of your income.

Don't say, "Sixty cents is no big deal." Add another few zeros and it starts to make a difference. Sixty cents of a dollar is 60%—more than half. In other words, if you earn $100 you have to pay $60 in taxes, if you earn $10,000 you have to pay $6,000 in taxes and if you earn $100,000, you have to pay $60,000 in taxes. Now do we have your attention?

Note that this situation is for taxpayers (that's all of us) that are in the 38% state and federal income "tax bracket" (that's many of us). Check with your accountant to find out in which combined state and federal tax bracket you are. With our nation's convoluted tax laws, the answer may not be simple.

Numbers count, so remember the math

Most people think that if they are in the 38% bracket, they have to earn $1.38 to keep $1.00. We wish that was true, but it's not.

Their math is wrong because it doesn't take into account the tax you have to pay on the extra 38¢. You need to earn 22¢ more to cover the tax you pay on the extra 38¢.

Illustration of after-tax income

Let's assume that you are in a combined state and federal tax bracket of 38%.

If you earn $1.60, you will have only $1.00 left:

$1.60	(Income before taxes)
x .38	(Tax bracket rate)
$ .608	(Tax paid)

That means, on every $1.60 you earn, you have to pay a little more than $.60 in taxes, leaving you with only $1.00.

$1.60	(Taxable income)
−.60	(Minus the tax, rounded to 60¢)
1.00	(After-tax income)

You can calculate it from the other direction:

If you earn $1.00, you will get to keep only 62¢ when the combined federal and state income tax rate is 38%.

38% of the total is tax

100 − 38% = 62% (what is left after taxes)

The above figures are rounded to the nearest cent.

Remember: saving is easier than earning

The good news is that every dollar that you save is equivalent to earning $1.60. Decide for yourself. Is it easier for you to go out and earn $160 so you can spend $100? Or is it easier to simply save the $100 (which is equivalent to having $160)? Obviously, it's easier to save the $100.

Tax avoidance vs. tax evasion

Everyone who wants to truly become wealthy needs to understand the difference between tax avoidance and tax evasion. Tax avoidance is taking advantage of all legal planning methods to reduce your taxes. It is legal to eliminate paying taxes that you are not obligated to pay. A qualified accountant can assist you in reducing your taxes to the legal minimum.

On the other hand, tax evasion is illegal. Examples include not reporting all of your income, misrepresenting your income, or deliberately putting income into the wrong category. Tax evasion is punished by fines and penalties and possible imprisonment. Furthermore, none of that looks good on your record. In short: don't even think about evading any of the taxes legally required of you.

Constitutional arguments against paying income tax are scams. Always file your income tax returns.

Most gains are taxed on a federal and state level and sometimes on a more local basis (some cities have income tax). Find out what your income tax bracket is and the effect these taxes will have on you.

Tax credits vs. tax deductions

A tax credit is worth $1.00 for every dollar of credit. That means that you are entitled to the full amount of the credit against the tax to be paid. You gain a 100% savings from a tax credit.

A tax deduction merely reduces income and therefore reduces that amount of income on which you have to pay taxes. The worth of a tax deduction varies, depending on your tax bracket. Consult with your financial counselor or your accountant about the difference between tax credits and tax deductions.

Use your deductions

There are many techniques for reducing taxes, including charitable deductions. The tax laws change yearly, so check with your accountant before you plan a charitable deduction. Review any tax-reducing activities with a qualified financial planner and accountant to make sure you are being tax-wise with your spending, investing, and savings.

In order to receive all the deductions to which you are entitled, keep all receipts for items that result in tax deductions or tax credits. You need to have the appropriate information for the preparation of your tax return. Also, you would be asked to have documentation of the expenses in case of an audit.

Get professional help

Have a tax professional prepare or review your tax return. If you file a simple tax return, capable advice is readily available. Veterans have access to tax services through the Veteran's Administration. Many community-based organizations have tax preparation volunteers or know where to get tax advice for you. More complex returns may require a qualified accountant experienced in preparing returns to review them. They could save you a lot of money. Be sure to inquire about their qualifications.

To research qualified accountants in your area, look in the yellow pages phone directory or search online at sites such as **www.searchforaccountants.com**, **www.accountants.com** and **www.cpadirectory. com**.

> *It's not if you owe;*
> *it's how much you owe.*

Chapter 22

INVESTING WISELY

"Money is like manure; it's not worth a thing
unless it's spread around encouraging young things to grow."
—Thornton Wilder

When you establish the habit of saving, you will be able to start investing what you have saved. There are many dreams that you thought were out of reach, but they are obtainable under a good investment plan. What do you need to do to improve your career and your earning capacity? Plan ahead to create a legacy for your loved ones that lasts for future generations. You can do that by investing wisely in real estate and stocks and establishing businesses. You must also protect your investments, your home, and the value of your income through proper insurance.

Use your money wisely

Money is magic. If you don't believe this, think about the power money has to multiply and magnetize. Money multiplies and magnetizes good, if good is already happening. More money will make the good greater. The opposite also is true: Money multiplies and magnetizes bad, if bad is already happening. More money will make the bad greater.

To illustrate, think about receiving a large inheritance. If you are someone who gives to charities, you will increase your giving. The money increases the good. If you are someone who is addicted to drugs and gambling, that's where the money will go. The money increases the bad.

Money has wings. It can appear and disappear right before our eyes. It has super-power energy to make us happy or sad. It can build great structures and then tear them down. Money is a form of energy that we give power to and then exchange that power and make its power flow from one person to another, from one entity to another, either for good or for bad.

Make interest your friend

Interest works 24/7/365. Is interest working for you—or for someone else? The answer is easy. Interest is working for you if you have investments. It is working against you if have debt. That's because debt takes money from you and gives it to others. Here's the winning strategy: Make interest your friend, make it work for you, not against you!

Compounded interest takes small amounts and makes them large amounts over time by paying interest on the interest. If you save even modest amounts over as little as fifteen to twenty years, that savings can create financial independence for the rest of your life. Earning interest helps you the same way that owing interest hurts you.

Spend on items that increase your wealth

Buy things that will appreciate in value and pay you back. This makes more sense than buying things that decrease in value and cost you more money, i.e., clothes and cars. Investments like real estate eventually increase in value over time. Just as importantly, real estate can offer more tax advantages than other investments.

An investment in your earning potential pays you back. You can invest in your career by spending on advanced training, tools, software, and the appropriate wardrobe that increase your potential for advancement. Be realistic about what will actually pay you back.

Cautiously keep your funds invested

Financial independence can be attained by successful investments. Investing is how you make compound interest work for you, not against you. To invest, you first need to have a small amount of capital. Other books will explain how to expand and leverage your capital. This book only tells you how to acquire the funds you need so you can invest.

Money that is not earning money is losing its value every day because of inflation. When it comes to inflation, it is true that "time is money." Money has to keep working to maintain its purchasing power. Money grows over time if promptly invested, even conservatively, because of the power of compound interest.

Let's say you have an investment that produces 6% a year in cash flow and a 4% appreciation for a total return of about 10%. What would you rather do with $1,000? Spend it on impulse items that may give you temporary pleasure and then be discarded (like expensive clothing that goes out of style or vacation trips that are soon forgotten)? Or would you rather invest in something that earns you $100 a year on average or more for the rest of your life and that you can pass on to your heirs or enjoy later in life?

You could let the $100 compound over time, that is, reinvest the income. At 10% compounded, an investment doubles about every seven years. For a young person with decades of work years until retirement, that $1,000 doubling every seven years might become an asset worth $32,000 or more.

This assumes that the money is invested in a growth asset in which there is no income tax during the growth of the asset. Distributions, if any, may be covered by depreciation. If you don't know how to do this, talk to a qualified accountant or qualified financial consultant.

Avoid risky investments

When you hear about a so-called "hot" investment, here's an easy test. It's called the "Would you want this to appear on the front page of the local newspaper?" test. Another test is the "Would you be proud to introduce your new business partner to your mother?" test.

Could this risky venture you're considering "blow up" and cause you shame? If you're worried, stop and think. If a deal sounds "too good to be true," unfortunately, it probably is not true at all—and could lead to heartache and embarrassment.

Choose "hard now, easy later"

Believe in yourself but recognize your limitations. Listen to people who warn you to be careful. They can help protect you from possible risk. There are always problems of some sort so plan for them. Know that you will have to make some sacrifices and accept some discomfort and inconvenience along the way in order to make calculated risks pay off.

Sometimes a good deal is worth a great deal of effort. It is worth a bit of sacrifice now, for greater gain later. A small amount of hard now can result in a lot of easy later. The reverse is true, too—a small amount of easy now can result in a lot of hard later.

Remember: Timing is everything

Always be prepared for opportunity. You never know when it might appear.

Several years ago Sam met a young man seated next to him on an airplane. The young man shared with him that he had a great idea for a business, but no capital. Many businesses start out adequately capitalized but waste their funds in the early stages of the enterprise. When they reach their growth period, they have burned-up their cash and run into financial trouble. Sam offered to fund the enterprise if the young man's business plan proved to be solid.

Sam's new partner started working out of his apartment, with one truck. Now he has more than seventeen trucks. The business has grown from breaking even at $600,000 in sales the first year, to now over $3.5 million, with a profit margin of over 15%.

Sam and this partner were prepared for the opportunity when it came to them. Through good timing, they took a small start and turned it into big gains.

Don't overlook your long-term perspective

Does your budget have an "end-game"? What are you saving for in the long run? You can't reach your goal until you know where the goal is.

One way to get an overall perspective on your finances is to use a process called LEAP. LEAP stands for the Lifetime Economic Acceleration Process. LEAP practitioners in your area can meet with you at no charge to integrate your finances and coordinate your overall strategy. They can help you achieve your full financial potential using a computer simulator that explores all of your options and verifies the outcomes, free of any bias or opinions. We believe that LEAP is an excellent way to strategize your financial future. You can find out more about LEAP at **www.leapsystems.com.**

Understand your home as a debt

The biggest debt that most consumers have is their home loan. Your home is your castle. Hopefully, you didn't buy more castle than you can afford.

You may have assumed that the value of your home would never drop. Maybe you were hoping that your income would increase so that you could afford the higher payments. Maybe you forgot to add in the cost of maintenance, insurance, and taxes on your house. For whatever reasons, many people fool themselves into buying more house than they can comfortably afford.

Hang onto your home

If you bought your home with an adjustable-rate mortgage (ARM), the interest rate on your loan may be resetting to a higher rate soon. If you have an ARM, make an appointment as soon as possible with your home loan provider. Assure them that you will work with them closely to keep your home. Get a printout of your reset mortgage estimate, including what your new monthly mortgage will be and when it will start. If the reset rate is higher, you will have to pay more each month to keep your home. Start preparing for this new expense immediately.

If you have good credit and want to avoid the uncertainty of adjustable interest rates, you can try to refinance your home with a fixed interest rate. In a time of tight mortgage credit, however, this can be more difficult to do. If you need to refinance and you can't find a new loan, ask your lender for help. Document your efforts.

Avoid foreclosure

Many homes across the country are going into foreclosure. If you are afraid that you can no longer pay your home mortgage, you may be facing foreclosure, too. Whatever you do, try to stay in your home.

Here are some online resources to help you prevent foreclosure:

- **www.hud.gov/foreclosure** (800-569-4287). HUD is the U.S. Department of Housing and Urban Development. This site lists HUD-certified credit and foreclosure prevention counseling agencies.
- **www.housing.org** (888-331-3332). Project Sentinel is a local HUD-certified counseling agency.
- **www.nhssv.org** (408-279-2600). Neighborhood Housing Services Silicon Valley is another local HUD-certified counseling agencies.
- **www.homeloanlearningcenter.com**. Mortgage Bankers Associations Home Loan Learning Center has information under Your Finances, then Foreclosure and Delinquency.
- **www.995hope.org** (888-995-HOPE). This is the site for Homeownership Preservation Foundation.

Save on your property insurance

You may be able to save on your property insurance. Property insurance companies often sell their client data to each other. If this happens to you, you could possibly be charged higher rates and offered lower coverage due to a previous claim. An "insurance score," similar to a credit score or rating, is often assigned without the client's knowledge.

Find out what your insurance score report says and if it includes any errors. Request your free copy at **www.choicetrust.com** and **www.iso.com** (under the link "useful features").

Save on your property taxes

You may be able to save on your property taxes. If your home has dropped in value, you may be able to petition your county tax board to reassess your home and tax you at its current, lower value. File the request for reduction in your property tax assessment by contacting your county assessor's office. They will ask you a few simple questions such as your contact information, parcel number of your house, and your estimation of what the current value of your house might be. It's not necessary to hire someone to file the request for you.

Understand assets versus liabilities

To put it simply, some assets are possessions that add to your wealth. (Let's call them "cows," because they give milk.) Other assets can actually take wealth away. (Let's call them "alligators," because they take a big bite out of your income.) Some possessions look like cows, but actually, they are alligators. The goal is to raise cows and not to tame alligators.

An example of an alligator is your car. Yes, a car is considered an asset, because it is something you own. But it is not a real cow because it doesn't earn you money (unless you are in the taxi or limousine business). It is like an alligator because it costs you money to maintain and fill with gas. Also, the value of the car decreases with every year and every mile.

Your home is probably increasing in value as a long-term investment. In that way, it's an asset, or cow. But you have locked up a huge investment of your funds into your home. There is a "lost opportunity cost" on that money. (That is the cost you "paid" because you couldn't invest the money in ways that made a higher profit.) Also, your house consumes income for maintenance, improvements, taxes, insurance, etc. In that way, your house is a liability or an alligator.

A clearer example is renting the place where you live, rather than buying it. Renting is seldom good use of your money. It is an alligator because it takes and doesn't give.

A good mental exercise is to examine all the ways you could use your money. For example, what you could have done with the funds you invested in a house if you hadn't purchased it? Are you sure that your home value going to increase faster than the money you could have made if you had invested it somewhere else? It never hurts to ask. See the Suggested Reading list at the end of this book and Robert Kiyosaki's book, *Rich Dad, Poor Dad* for more thoughts on this.

To recap, buy cows that beef up your wallet, not alligators that chew it up.

**It's not the alligators;
it's the cows that create wealth.**

Chapter 23

FOLLOW THE PRINCIPLES OF FINANCIAL INDEPENDENCE

"Life is not about having and getting,
but about being and becoming."
—Matthew Arnold

A Silicon Valley billionaire named David Cheriton made his fortune as a professor when he offered to nurture the concept of a start-up company, even though it had an odd name. The name of the company? Google. Cheriton attributes much of his success to "resourceful use of economic goods and services in order to achieve lasting and more fulfilling goals."

We like his attitude that resourcefulness and fulfillment are part of the big picture. Over the past fifty years, Sam has been resourceful in achieving financial independence. This has allowed him to pursue increasingly fulfilling goals. If you learn resourcefulness by following his principles listed below, your life will become more fulfilled, too.

SAM'S PRINCIPLES OF FINANCIAL INDEPENDENCE

1. **Daily choices add up**. How you spend your money now determines what you will have in the future. It takes many "daily" bricks to build the financial fortress that will protect you for a lifetime.

2. **Small savings over a long time creates more wealth than big risks.** Slow and study wins the race. The turtle will outrun the hare. Small savings continuously made over a period of time are more likely to create substantial wealth than taking big risks. Remember the miracle of compound interest.

3. **Pay yourself first.** Your savings should be your primary goal. To make sure that your savings account gets paid, pay it first. Take your savings portion off the top of your income, not the bottom of your income. What is left over is what you live on, day to day.

4. **Separate wants from needs. Concentrate on needs.** Distinguish between wants and needs. Until you're financially independent, concentrate solely on needs.

5. **Toxic debt is poison.** It constricts your financial wellbeing by burdening you with interest payments and dependence on further debt. Toxic debt also prevents you from investing and achieving your financial goals.

6. **Credit is for emergencies. Pay cash until you reach your goal.** Until you are financially independent, use credit only for emergencies. Only buy that for which you can pay cash.

7. **Windfalls are capital, not income. Capital is for wealth investment**. Surplus cash and windfalls, such as bonuses, financial gifts, etc., are capital not income. Capital is for making investments that will produce income or increase wealth.

8. **Never take a risk or purchase an item you cannot afford.** Calculate if the risk or the purchase will keep you awake at night. Remember, if you are careful now, you will be able to afford more things you want eventually.

9. **Put your own oxygen mask on first.** When it comes to giving, you must put your own oxygen mask on first. You can't help others if you're not okay yourself.

10. **Inexpensive gifts can show you care. Expensive gifts give a false impression and are motivated by insecurity.** The purpose of a gift is to show you care. An overly expensive gift can give a false impression and indicate insecurity. What is expensive is relative, depending on your income.

11. **Enjoyment of luxury is brief. But the anxiety can last a long time, at least until the debt is paid.** The pleasure you get from buying a luxury item is short-lived (usually just a few days or weeks). But the anxiety and insecurity caused by the debt go deeper and last longer.

12. **Get fulfillment from personal relationships, not material things**. Love people and use things; don't love things and use people.

13. **Why are you shopping? Know the reasons**. This will help you make better decisions. Don't shop because you feel bored or insecure.

14. **Resist the urge to indulge in instant gratification. Invest instead.** Resist seeking satisfaction from impulse purchases, even if they are small. Whenever the desire strikes, pay down debt or set the amount aside to invest instead.

15. **Ask, ask, ask for what you want—and be clear.** You never know how someone will respond. A manager may give you a discount. Your spouse/significant other may fulfill your desires. Make your needs known, and you may be happily surprised.

16. **Comparison shop first.** Check out the competition. Make sure you are getting the best value and what you really want for the funds that you have available.

17. **Buy wholesale whenever possible.** Make the slightly longer trip to a wholesale district or a discount store. Depending on what the item is, the savings can be significant.

18. **Do not buy labels, buy value.** What you want is quality and value, not status labels. Most people won't know if you are wearing a designer item, because they won't see the designer label inside your garment. An item doesn't increase in value just because a famous name is attached to it. This holds true for other things, such as jewelry, furniture, tableware, linens and cars.

19. **Buy pre-owned whenever appropriate.** A car depreciates by thousands of dollars the moment it is taken out of the showroom. Few people notice whether an item is pre-owned or not. Also, you can often get better quality at a much lower price at garage sales and auctions.

20. **Keep price tags, receipts and packaging.** Keep original packaging, receipts and price tags

on your purchases until you are sure you really want the item. Maybe a pushy sales person or a so-called friend convinced you to buy it. Perhaps the item is defective, doesn't fit your need, or costs more than you can really afford. You may even find the same item the next day for substantially less or a better item for less (see #16). Keep your options open.

21. **Keep your funds invested and working for you, but cautiously.** Money that is not earning money is losing its value every day because of inflation. Money has to keep working to maintain its purchasing power. Money properly invested, even conservatively, grows over time because of the power of compound interest.

22. **Income $1.00; spend 99¢ = happiness; spend $1.01 = misery.** If you spend less than you earn you will be happier. If you spend more than you earn you will become anxious. Overspending puts you into debt. Before you know it, you're working in the future to pay for things that you enjoyed in the past.

23. **Buy what pays you; don't buy things that decrease in value or cost to own.** What pay you back are financial investments and investments in yourself, such as the necessary education, training, wardrobe, tools, and equipment to advance your career. Don't invest in things that don't increase in value, advance your career or pay you back.

24. **Immediately set aside for taxes.** Do not forget taxes when you get a bonus. When you make a profit or commission, immediately set aside the amount that will be required to pay the tax.

25. **Personal purchases cost you 60% more because they are after tax**. This is the 60% rule: You are actually paying 60% more than the stated price because you are buying with your after-tax income.
26. **It's not how much you make—IT'S HOW MUCH YOU KEEP**. We all know people who make a lot of money but don't have anything. People who have modest incomes can become very wealthy by hanging onto their money.

Below is a shorter version of these principles. We urge you to copy this list and post it on your bathroom mirror, your refrigerator, or your car visor. Read the list every morning and night until these principles becomes a permanent part of your thinking.

SAM'S PRINCIPLES OF FINANCIAL INDEPENDENCE

1. **Daily choices add up**.
2. **Small savings over a long time create more wealth than big risks.**
3. **Pay yourself first.**
4. **Separate wants from needs. Concentrate on needs.**
5. **Toxic debt is poison.**
6. **Credit is for emergencies. Pay cash until you reach your goal.**
7. **Windfalls are capital, not income. Capital is for wealth investment.**
8. **Never take a risk or purchase an item you cannot afford.**
9. **Put your own oxygen mask on first.**

10. **Inexpensive gifts can show you care. Expensive gifts give a false impression and are motivated by insecurity.**
11. **Enjoyment of luxury is brief. But the anxiety can last a long time, at least until the debt is paid.**
12. **Get fulfillment from personal relationships not material things.**
13. **Why are you shopping? Know the reasons.**
14. **Resist the urge to indulge in instant gratification; invest instead.**
15. **Ask, ask, ask for what you want —and be clear.**
16. **Comparison shop first.**
17. **Buy wholesale whenever possible.**
18. **Do not buy labels, buy value.**
19. **Buy pre-owned whenever appropriate.**
20. **Keep price tags and receipts.**
21. **Keep your funds invested and working for you, but cautiously.**
22. **Income $1.00; spend 99¢ = happiness; spend $1.01 = misery.**
23. **Buy what pays you; don't buy things that decrease in value or cost to own.**
24. **Immediately set aside for taxes.**
25. **Personal purchases cost you 60% more because they are after tax.**
26. **It's not how much you make—IT'S HOW MUCH YOU KEEP.**

CONCLUSION

Now it's time to close the circle. We started with your personal relationship with money, and shared some ways that you can make a difference in your savings plan. We looked at how the world deals with your money. Finally, we want you to take a closer look at your own life, as it relates to "the big picture."

This book is intended to help strengthen your determination to reach financial independence. When you become financially independent, you won't be as focused on getting and spending money. Instead, you'll be free to focus on where your life fits into the rest of your world.

When you gain financial independence, you start to realize that the world isn't "all about you." There are other people on the planet, too. Take a moment to think about those around you that you could help if you had a bountiful supply of funds. Dream about what you would like to do to make the world a better place.

After you learn to hang onto your dough, make your dough rise! Use your money to create a truly meaningful life. What is it that you want to become? What would you like to do to make a difference, if money were no longer a concern? There are endless opportunities for philanthropy and helping others. As Winston Churchill said, "We make a living by what we get, but we make a life by what we give."

Remember to visit our website **www. TheSmartestWay.com** often for tips, encouragement, updates, and a provocative blog.

Please email us and tell us how things are coming along for you!

Remember....
It's not how much you make;
  it's how much you keep.
It's not your income that makes you rich;
  it's your savings habits.
It's not what your money makes of you;
  it's what you make of your money.
It's not how much you own;
  it's how little you owe.
It's not the "have-to"s or "want-to"s;
  it's the "need-to"s.
It's not what you do;
  it's how you do it.
It's not your habits that control you;
  it's you who controls your habits.
It's not the wishing;
  it's the doing.
It's not the credit card that is the master;
  you are the master.
It's not what you start with;
  it's what you end with.
It's not what you spend together;
  it's how you spend together.
It's not how much you spend for your children;
  it's how much you care for your children.
It's now how much you spend on a gift;
  it's what you give and how you give it.
It's not what you own;
  it's who you are.
It's not what you drive;
  it's what you pay for what you drive.
It's not your wealth;
  it's your health.
It's not how much you spend for fun;
  it's how much fun you have.

It's not what you buy;
  it's how you shop.
It's not where you shop;
  it's what you get.
It's not what you wear;
  it's what you pay for what you wear.
It's not what you know;
  it's what you don't know.
It's not if you owe;
  it's how much you owe.
It's not the alligators;
  it's the cows that create wealth.

About the Authors

Sam Freshman has dedicated his professional life to being an attorney, banker, business owner, real estate developer, investor, author, and lecturer. He has been Adjunct Professor of Real Estate Law at the Graduate School of Business at University of Southern California. He has lectured extensively on real estate investments at Stanford University, Pepperdine University, University of Southern California, University of California Los Angeles, Bar Associations and CPA Societies.

In 1961, he formed Standard Management Co., which has sponsored hundreds of millions of dollars of investments in real estate projects throughout the country. His book *Principles of Real Estate Syndication* (3rd edition, 2006, Beverly Hills Publishing Co.) is considered the landmark work on the subject and carries more than twenty "five-star" reviews on Amazon.com.

In recent years, he has devoted a substantial portion of his time to mentoring graduate students and young professionals. He has become an expert on behavioral attitudes that create success. Attendees of his seminars pay up to $5,000 to hear him speak and consult with him. Sam has four daughters and seven grandchildren and lives with his wife Ardyth in Beverly Hills, California. You can find out more about Sam at **www.standardmanagement.com** and **www.syndicationideas.com**.

Heidi Clingen has a twenty-five-year background in journalism, editing and writing. Her journalistic experience includes staff titles and editor positions at fashion trade and consumer publications including *The Apparel News Group* in Los Angeles and *The Wall Street Journal* in New York, where she received a Dow Jones Foundation Fellowship. Heidi holds a bachelor's degree in journalism, magna cum laude, from San Francisco State University; a certificate in grant writing from The Grantsmanship Center Institute in Los Angeles; and a certificate in screenwriting from University of California, Los Angeles.

Heidi has two sons and lives with her husband Bill in Valencia, California. You can find out more about Heidi at **www.allwritey.com**.

OUR MISSION STATEMENT
for "TheSmartestWay to Succeed" Series™

To help you find smarter, easier ways
to succeed in all areas of your life.

A Note to Our Readers

Dear Reader,

Success takes a great amount of time and effort!

That's why we are creating *TheSmartestWay* to Succeed Series™. Our easy-to-read books are filled with quick chunks of powerful things to think about and tips you can start using today. There's something for everyone in every book.

We want to hear from you! We want you to succeed in life *TheSmartestWay*. Has this book been helpful? Please email your comments to: **Heidi@TheSmartestWay.com.**

May true success be yours,

Sam Freshman and Heidi Clingen

Be a part of "*TheSmartestWay*™ to Save More"!

We are already writing
the second volume of this book!
Please email us your favorite tips
and stories
on how to save money.
If we use your suggestions in
"*TheSmartestWay*™ to Save More,"
we will send you two copies of the book,
one for you and one for a friend!

Want us to speak to your group?

We create customized workshops for groups
to share how to do things *TheSmartestWay*™ !

Want to meet us in person?

We offer confidential, private coaching sessions
to help make *TheSmartestWay*™ philosophy a
part of your life.

Contact us!

Email: Heidi@TheSmartestWay.com
Phone: (888-524-8833).

Want to invest your savings?–Read this book!

Principles of Real Estate Syndication 3rd Edition
By Samuel K. Freshman

Known throughout the real estate industry as the definitive "how-to," *Principles of Real Estate Syndication* is filled with examples and illustrations of all aspects of buying property with others. This reference guide thoroughly explains the theory and practice of this exciting way to invest.

Here is what some of the more than twenty "five-star" reviews on **www.amazon.com** say about the book:

"...This book could be titled, *How to Build a Real Estate Empire*. The book provides practical information and advice on avoiding common mistakes...."

"...comprehensive and authoritative—a must read for anyone who contemplates investing in a syndication or becoming a syndicator ... a treasure trove of information...."

"...a hands-on book, well-written, easy to comprehend, and offers the reader a strategic insight into a complex business form ... should be a permanent fixture in every office...."

"...This is *the* instruction manual for this type of venture—a compelling synthesis of practical and technical advice and legal analysis. I recommend the book to anyone involved in real estate or other syndications—attorneys, accountants, bankers, investors, syndicators, students and more...."

"...If you are serious about making money in real estate, read this book. ... This book explains in simple and easy to understand language the preparation, execution and practices that must be taken to become successful in the field...."

"...I truly believe this book, if properly followed, can make anybody who reads it substantial amounts of money .... There are dozens of real estate investing books out there, but this is clearly the best I've found...."

Samuel K. Freshman has a distinguished career in real estate and law both as an advisor and investment partner. He is past Chairman of the Legal and Accounting Committee of the California Real Estate Association Syndication Division. He assisted in the preparation of the California Corporation and Real Estate Commissioner's syndicate regulations. In 1961 he formed Standard Management Co., which has sponsored hundreds of millions of dollars of investments in real estate projects throughout the country.

You can purchase *Principles of Real Estate Syndication, 3rd Edition* by Samuel K. Freshman at **www.amazon.com**, **www.barnesandnoble.com** or **www.syndicationideas.com.**

SUGGESTED READING

BUDGETING:

Straight Talk on Money: Ken and Daria Dolan's Guide to Family Money Management, Ken and Daria Dolan, Simon & Shuster, New York, New York, 1993.

1001 Ways to Cut Your Expenses, Jonathan D. Pond, Dell Publishing, a division of Bantam Doubleday Dell Publishing Group, New York, New York, 1992.

365 Ways to Save Money, Lucy H. Hedrick, William Morrow & Co., New York, New York, 1994.

Financial Fitness in 45 Days: The Complete Guide to Shaping Up Your Personal Finances, Lorayne Fiorillo, Entrepreneur Media Inc., Irvine, California, 2000.

The Expert Consumer, A Complete Handbook, Kenneth Eisenberger, Prentice Hall, Inglewood Cliffs, New Jersey, 1997.

Getting the Most for Your Money: How to Beat the High Cost of Living, Anthony Scaduto, Paperback Library, a division of Coronet Communications, Inc. New York, New York, 1977.

Secondhand Is Better, Douglas Matthews, Suzanne Wymelenberg and Susan Cheever Cowley, Arbor House Publishing Co., New York, New York, 1975.

Save Your Money, Save Your Face, What Every Cosmetics Buyer Needs to Know, Elaine Brumberg and Julie Coopersmith, Facts on File Publications, New York, New York, 1989.

Life without Debt: Free Yourself from the Burden of Money Worries Once and for All, Bob Hammond, Career Press, Franklin Lakes, New Jersey, 1995.

Take This Book to the Hospital with You: a Consumer Guide to Surviving Your Hospital Stay, Charles B. Inlander and Ed Weiner, People's Medical Society, Allentown, Pennsylvania, 1993.

MONEY AND RELATIONSHIPS:

Women, Men & Money: The Four Keys for Using Money to Nourish Your Relationship, Bankbook and Soul, William Francis Devine, Jr., Harmony Books, a division of Crown Publishers, Inc., New York, New York, 1998.

The Seven Stages of Money Maturity: Understanding the Spirit and Value of Money in Your Life, George Kinder, Delacorte Press, a division of Random House, New York, New York, 1999.

The Advisor's Guide to Money Psychology: Taking the Fear Out of Financial Decision- Making, 2nd Ed., Olivia Mellan with Sherry Christie, Investment Advisor Press, Shrewsbury, New Jersey, 2004.

If I Think About Money So Much, Why Can't I Figure It Out? Understanding and Overcoming Your Money Complex, Arlene Modica Matthews, Summit Books, New York, New York, 1991.

WOMEN AND MONEY:

Power Tools for Women in Business: 10 Ways to Succeed in Life and Work, Aliza Sherman, Entrepreneur Media Inc., Irvine, California, 2001.

What Every Woman Should Know about Her Husband's Money, Shelby White, Turtle Bay Books, a division of Random House, New York, New York, 1992.

INVESTING:

The Only Investment Guide You'll Ever Need, Andrew Tobias, Harcourt Books, Orlando, Florida, 2005.

Rich Dad, Poor Dad: What the Rich Teach Their Kids About Money—That the Poor and Middle Class Do Not! Robert T. Kiyosaki with Sharon L. Lechter, C.P.A., Warner Books, New York, New York, 1998.

MAGAZINES

Barron's
www.barrons.com
Best Life
www.bestlifeonline.com
Better Homes & Gardens (family money section)
www.bhg.com
Business Week
www.businessweek.com
Consumer Reports
www.consumerreports.com
Forbes
www.forbes.com
Fortune
www.cnnmoney.com
Good Housekeeping
www.goodhousekeeping.com
Kiplinger's Personal Finance
www.kiplinger.com/magazine
Money
www.cnnmoney.com
Real Simple
www.realsimple.com
Shopping Smart
www.smartshoppingmag.com
Smart Money
www.smartmoney.com
USA Today
www.usatoday.com/money
US News & World Report (money and business section)
www.usnews.com
Worth
www.worth.com
Young Money
www.youngmoney.com

MY PERSONAL ACTION PLAN

I will START:

_____
_____
_____
_____
_____
_____
_____
_____
_____

I will STOP:

_____
_____
_____
_____
_____
_____
_____
_____
_____

I will RECOMMEND to others:

_____
_____
_____
_____
_____
_____
_____
_____
_____

Want to receive our FREE email tips,
"TheSmartestWay **to Succeed™"?**

Sign up at:

www.TheSmartestWay.com
or
tips@TheSmartestWay.com
or
Fill out this form and fax it to **(661-255-6451).**

Name _____

Email address _____

Where did you find this book? _____